$\mathcal{M}$ORE THAN

PETTICOATS

REMARKABLE
VIRGINIA
$\mathcal{W}$OMEN

MORE THAN PETTICOATS SERIES

MORE THAN
PETTICOATS

———◆———

REMARKABLE
VIRGINIA
WOMEN

Emilee Hines

TWODOT®

GUILFORD, CONNECTICUT
HELENA, MONTANA
AN IMPRINT OF THE GLOBE PEQUOT PRESS

A · T W O D O T® · B O O K

Cover photo courtesy of Thomas B. Cantieri.

Library of Congress Cataloging-in-Publication Data

Hines, Emilee.
    More than petticoats : remarkable Virginia women / Emilee Hines.—1st ed.
        p. cm.— (More than petticoats series)
    Includes bibliographical references (p.) and index
ISBN 0-7627-2364-5
I. Women—Virginia—Biography. 2. Women—Virginia—History. 3. Texas—
    Biography.
I. Title: Remarkable Virginia women. II. Title. III. Series.

    CT3260.H56 2003
    920.72'09755—dc21
[B]   2002044702

Manufactured in the United States of America
First Edition/First Printing

I dedicate this book to
my sister Margaret Hines;
my daughter, Catherine Cantieri;
my niece, Elizabeth Price;
and to the memory of my mother,
Margaret Ferguson Hines
and my sister Iris Humphrey,
all remarkable Virginia women.

CONTENTS

ᴀCKNOWLEDGMENTS

In any work requiring research, librarians are essential. I wish to thank the staff of the Kirn Memorial Library in Norfolk and the staff of Portsmouth Public Library, both the Churchland Branch and the Main Branch. I especially thank Jeannette Tomso, who was able to acquire books for me through interlibrary loan and who helped me locate sources of material I wasn't aware of.

I'd also like to thank my husband Thomas B. Cantieri, and also Sara Hines Martin, Becky and Ernest Bowling, Jerry Catron, Lucy and Jim Alexander, Nancy Leasure of the Washington County Historical Society, Marian Payne, and Irene Stanley.

Thanks go also to my editor, Charlene Patterson, who improves manuscripts with gentle critiquing.

And though I can no longer tell them in person, I'd like to thank my parents for assuring me that a woman can become whatever she wants to be.

$\mathcal{I}$NTRODUCTION

As Americans, we owe a great debt to the remarkable group of Founding Fathers who were able to create a nation from thirteen quarrelsome colonies and then to make that nation grow and prosper. We also owe much to an equally remarkable group, the Founding Mothers, who made it possible for these men to go off to battle, to hammer out a constitution, and to conduct business. Many of these women shaped our country through their own work as writers, religious leaders, politicians, philanthropists, bankers, and even spies. You'll meet some of these remarkable ladies in this book.

Some of the outstanding women of Virginia were born to wealth and privilege; others worked their way up from poverty or overcame illness and legal obstacles to achieve their goals. The women profiled here represent the three races prevalent in Virginia's history: Native American, European, and African American. Many of them were related by blood or knew each other from working together. For example, Dolley Madison and Madame Russell were cousins; Edith Bolling Wilson was a descendant of Pocahontas; Maggie Walker's mother had been a slave in Elizabeth Van Lew's home.

Virginians probably owe more to Pocahontas than to any other man or woman. She was able to establish friendships with the Jamestown colonists across racial and cultural lines. Without her help, the colony might have failed.

Fourteen significant Virginia women are described in this volume. There easily could have been many more: women who ran businesses, established schools and museums, even one imaginative young lady who dressed as a man and took her father's place in jail until her ruse (and her gender) was discovered.

Some of these women had tragically short lives; others lived into their nineties. They are a diverse, interesting, significant group, and their stories should be inspiring to all.

POCAHONTAS

1596–1617

America's Princess

On an April day in 1613, Pocahontas walked the narrow plank leading onto the ship *Treasurer,* anchored in the Potomac River. She was accompanied by a Potowomeke chief, Jopassus, and his wife.

For more than three years, her father, King Powhatan, had forbidden her to have anything to do with the English settlers, and he'd sent her away from Jamestown to the far reaches of his domain. But she liked the English settlers and welcomed this chance to visit with Captain Samuel Argall and other Englishmen onboard the ship, which had sailed up Potomac River from Jamestown.

After the group had dinner, Jopassus and his wife took Pocahontas to the gunners' room of the ship, told her to wait a few minutes, and left her. Instead of returning, they disembarked with the copper kettle they'd been paid for luring her onto the vessel.

Time passed, and Pocahontas realized her companions were not coming back. Then the ship began to move. She was a prisoner.

Argall sailed with his hostage back to Jamestown, where Pocahontas was welcomed by settlers who had known her earlier and who

Pocahontas in her Elizabethan costume.

appreciated all she had done to save the colony of Virginia. The colony's governor, Sir Thomas Gates, sent word to Chief Powhatan that he held Pocahontas. She would be reunited with her father when the chieftain returned the Englishmen he'd captured, along with tools and other goods stolen from Jamestown. He must also make permanent peace with the English, cease warring against neighboring tribes, and furnish the settlers with corn if he wanted his daughter back.

Powhatan returned seven captured English settlers and sent the colony one canoe of corn, saying he'd send more after the fall harvest. He continued fighting against other tribes, however, and attacked the outlying areas of the Virginia settlement. He made no further efforts to ransom his daughter.

Pocahontas was sent to live near Henrico, Virginia. Reverend Alexander Whitaker and the women parishioners of his church took charge of her, teaching her the English language and English ways. Pocahontas would eventually bring about peace between the colonists and Indians, but in an unexpected way.

The famous Indian maiden was born at the chief settlement of the Powhatan tribe, Werowocomoco, in 1596 or 1597. She was named Matoaka, which meant "Little Snow Feather." Pocahontas, her nickname, has been translated by the English as "Bright Stream between Two Hills" and by the Powhatans as "Little Wanton."

Pocahontas's father had become chieftain in 1570 and had taken the tribe's name, Powhatan, as his own name. The Powhatans were part of the Algonquian nation. Ruthless and fierce, Powhatans conquered neighboring tribes, slaughtering the men and taking women and children captive. The tribe practiced torture and dismemberment of their enemies. Coming from this savage background, it is amazing that Pocahontas was able to become friends with the English and convert to their ways.

Chief Powhatan, an absolute dictator, had many wives, each of whom usually bore him only one child. Nothing is known of Pocahontas's mother. Powhatan may have given or sold her to another warrior, even to another tribe. She may have died in child-birth. Pocahontas, born when Powhatan was about fifty, was her father's favorite daughter.

Pocahontas was eleven or twelve when the first three shiploads of white settlers arrived at Jamestown, but this was not the first European incursion into Powhatan's territory. In 1560 the Spanish had captured a young Powhatan and taken him to Spain, where they'd educated and baptized him, calling him Don Luis. In

1570 they returned to the Chesapeake Bay area to set up a mission. Once back among the Powhatan, Don Luis reverted to his Native American ways and murdered the members of the expedition. The Spanish retaliated by hanging some innocent tribe members.

In 1585 the governor of Roanoke Island burned several villages in the southern part of Powhatan's domain. In 1604, just three years before Jamestown was established, a group of white men attempted to kidnap several Powhatan youths to sell as slaves in the Caribbean. When Powhatan warriors fought back, the whites shot and killed a number of them.

Thus, Powhatan and his people had good reason to mistrust the newly arrived English.

Pocahontas undoubtedly watched as the white-skinned people began building a fort, a storehouse, and a crude church. The settlers were shorter than Powhatan men, and by the native's standards, strangely dressed. While most Englishmen had beards, long hair, and often mustaches, the Powhatan men were clean-shaven and cut all but a single strip of hair across the top of their heads. They scraped their faces and scalps clean with sharpened shells. The Powhatans wore light moccasins or went barefoot; the English workmen wore heavy boots. The whites were called "coat wearers" because they wore several layers of long-sleeved clothing in all but the hottest weather. By contrast, the natives usually wore only small leather aprons or breechcloths that covered only a scant area of the body. Women and men alike went bare above the waist.

Pocahontas was interested in the tools and gadgets the Europeans brought. The Powhatans hunted with bows and arrows and spears, and clubbed their enemies with tomahawks. The killing portion of all these weapons was made of stones painstakingly chipped to sharpness. The natives shaped canoes by setting fire to logs and burning out the center portion. The English, on the other hand, had knives, axes, and saws to build with. They had brought glassblowers to Jamestown and soon were fashioning serviceable containers. Masons built kilns and burned bricks to build houses, replacing the first wooden ones.

Above all, the English had guns. Powhatan and his warriors had seen the effect of these weapons and wanted to steal some for themselves. Pocahontas looked on all the activity and strangeness with the awe of a child.

Among the colonists was twenty-six-year-old Captain John Smith. Already a veteran of the Turkish wars, he had been captured and made a slave, but he'd managed to escape while awaiting ransom. Despite the mistrust and jealousy of some of the colonists, Smith was one of the eight men chosen by the English king to govern the colony. Although he arrived in Jamestown in chains because of a disagreement onboard the ship, he was soon freed when the charter box was opened and the king's wishes were made known.

Perhaps because of his military experience in foreign lands, Smith recognized the need to communicate with the Native Americans. When he saw the girl watching, he welcomed her, and by means of signs and objects began to learn a few Powhatan words and to teach her some English words. He also gave her some of the gifts the London Company, sponsor of the expedition, had sent along: glass beads and a bell.

Although Powhatan was impressed with the English guns, they were ill-suited for fighting in Virginia. Too long and unwieldy for moving through the woods, they were also heavy and inconvenient to load and fire. While an Englishman was pouring in powder and shot and tamping it down, many arrows could speed toward their target. In addition, the English suits of armor were too hot and uncomfortable to work in, so the colonists rarely wore them, making themselves vulnerable to arrows and tomahawks. Several settlers were killed, and those remaining were afraid to go far outside the fort to hunt or fish.

In late June two of the three ships that had come to Jamestown returned to England, leaving the colonists with scant supplies. Disease and brackish water took their toll. By the end of the summer, half the colonists were dead.

Pocahontas noticed the Englishmen's distress and persuaded some friendly Powhatans to bring the settlers corn (maize). Her half brother Pochins brought corn and fish. Smith later told Queen Anne that Pocahontas saved the colony from death and starvation.

Smith realized the colony needed more food than Pocahontas could provide, knowing that at any time she could be prevented from bringing anything at all. He set out with three companions in early December 1607 to explore the Chicahominy River area and to find other natives who might supply food.

At a point near present-day Providence Forge, Smith went ashore with several native guides, leaving the other three men in the canoe. Within a few minutes he was set upon by Powhatan warriors. Using one of his guides as a shield, he backed away, but tumbled into an icy stream and was captured. Two of his fellow colonists were killed; the third was captured, dismembered, and his body was burned at the stake.

Smith was taken as a captive from one of Powhatan's brothers to the other. Each ruled a portion of the Powhatan empire. He was marched to the Rappahannock chief, who was to determine if Smith had been the one who kidnapped tribe members in 1604. If the chief had so identified him, Smith would have been killed. Finally he was taken before the high chieftain Powhatan himself, bound and helpless, realizing he was about to become the next torture/murder victim. Two great stones were brought forth, and Smith was stretched out with his head lying on one of them. Warriors gathered with clubs to beat him to death.

Suddenly Pocahontas came out of the crowd, put her arms around her friend's head, and laid her head down on his.

Powhatan honored a tradition and spared Smith's life. Smith was adopted into the tribe in a ceremony two days later, and then escorted back to Jamestown by twelve Powhatan warriors. Smith had promised Chief Powhatan several cannons at the fort, knowing the heavy weapons could not be lifted. He had also told the chieftain that the settlers were in Jamestown temporarily, taking refuge from the Spaniards.

Because she had saved him, Pocahontas was now, according to tradition, the guardian of Smith; his life was hers to do with as she wished.

Some historians have suggested that Pocahontas might have been disappointed that Smith did not marry her, but she was still a child by English standards. Others have said that Smith invented the story of his rescue. He was, however, the only survivor of the ill-fated exploration, and Pocahontas did spend a great deal of time in Jamestown during the next two years. Had there not been a special bond, Powhatan would undoubtedly have forbidden his daughter's relationship with Smith.

Pocahontas also often came to Jamestown to play with other native children, turning cartwheels, running races, and scampering about the settlement playing hide-and-seek.

Although still a child, Pocahontas was a princess who acted as a go-between for her father and the colonists. She reported to her father when a shipload of a hundred additional colonists arrived in January 1608, which contradicted Smith's claim that the settlers were only in Virginia temporarily. Powhatan sent for Smith and Captain Christopher Newport. When they went to see him, they took along a boy, Thomas Savage, who was to live with the Powhatans and learn their language; in return, a Powhatan warrior, Namontack, was to live at Jamestown.

Captain Newport traded far more liberally than Smith had, offering twenty swords for twenty turkeys. After Newport left, tribe members arrived with another twenty turkeys, but Smith refused to give them more swords. Smith took seven of them captive after they tried to steal the swords. Pocahontas was again the peacemaker, negotiating successfully for the return of the Powhatan warriors.

In the autumn of 1608, Smith was elected president of the council governing Jamestown. Food was plentiful, the church and storehouse were repaired, and things were going well.

When Captain Newport next visited Powhatan, he brought him a scarlet cloak and a European bed and other furniture. He also crowned Powhatan king of the Indians, despite Smith's objections. Smith thought all the generosity and elevation would make Powhatan more difficult to deal with, especially when the ship arrived with more hungry settlers late in the year. More food would be needed, and the growing season was past.

Smith was right. Powhatan now seemed more interested in fighting than trading, and when Smith tried to barter corn from the Nansemond tribe, he found that Powhatan had told them not to trade with the English. The chieftain seemed determined to get rid of the colonists. Before 1608 ended, Powhatan forbade Pocahontas to have anything to do with the English, or risk death. But she was twice more to aid the colony, putting her own life in jeopardy.

The situation at Jamestown grew desperate. The people were starving. Smith set off for Werowocomoco and talked with Powhatan, who was seated on his English bed surrounded by his wives and children, including Pocahontas. The two men argued about trade, weapons, and food. Refusing to disarm, Smith left before they could reach an agreement. Eventually Powhatan sent food to the barges and invited Smith back, but before the captain could leave the barge, Pocahontas arrived to warn him that her father planned to kill him at supper.

Meanwhile, despite Smith's instructions to the settlers to stay close to the fort, a group had gone hunting to Hog Island, their boat had capsized, and they had drowned. Richard Wiffen went to Werowocomoco to tell Smith of the tragedy. Powhatan warriors spotted Wiffen and were closing in to take him captive when Pocahontas grabbed him and hid him, sending the warriors searching in the opposite direction.

Smith strengthened the colony, but in July 1609, Captain Argall returned with news that the council had been abolished, a governor-for-life would soon arrive, and two of Smith's earlier enemies were returning to Virginia. Smith left Jamestown and began building a home farther upstream. He was on a boat carrying bags of gunpowder when it exploded, burning him badly.

Smith left Virginia for England in October 1609, and Pocahontas was told that he had died. Bereft of her best friend in Jamestown, she did not protest when her father sent her away to the northern reaches of his domain to live with his kin, the Patawomeke tribe.

The colony was thus without Smith and Pocahontas, two who had been responsible for the earlier peace and success. In an ambush later that year, Powhatan warriors killed sixty colonists. The remainder had little food, and that period in Virginia's colonial history is known as "The Starving Time." By spring 1610 only sixty remained of the 490 who had been in Jamestown the previous autumn. The survivors abandoned the settlement, boarded ships, and were sailing downriver on their way to England when the new governor, Sir Thomas Dale, arrived with food and determination.

Three years passed. The colony thrived and expanded, but the danger of attack always worried them. They thought if they could kidnap Pocahontas, they might force Powhatan to make peace. Captain Samuel Argall was sent in the *Treasurer* up the Chesapeake Bay to the Patawomekes. He bribed Jopassus and his wife to bring Pocahontas aboard the ship. The scheme worked, and the Indian princess was brought back to Jamestown.

Under the direction of the Reverend Alexander Whitaker and others, Pocahontas was taught Christianity. Although she could not read or write, she spoke English. She memorized portions of *The Book of Common Prayer*, expressed her faith, and was baptized in the spring of 1614 with the Christian name of Rebecca.

While at Henrico, eighteen-year-old Pocahontas met a widowed farmer named John Rolfe, ten years her senior. Rolfe and his wife had been shipwrecked in Bermuda on the way to Jamestown in 1610. Both their newborn child and Mrs. Rolfe died before reaching Virginia.

Rolfe was interested in growing tobacco, and Pocahontas showed him how the natives cultivated the crop. He saw the attractive maiden not only at work, but at church as well. Rolfe fell in love with Pocahontas, despite their differences.

In 1614 Rolfe wrote Governor Dale, asking permission to marry Pocahontas. He detailed all the reasons against the marriage: her lack of education, her barbaric background, the long-standing taboo against a mixed marriage, even the Biblical admonition against marrying "strange wives." Still, he wrote, he was besotted with her. He assured the governor that the marriage would not be for carnal reasons only, but for the good of the colony and for the good of his soul.

Dale quickly agreed to the marriage. Perhaps this would be just the thing to heal relations between the two races. He accompanied Rolfe and Pocahontas on a visit to Powhatan, who sent two of his sons to meet them. Pocahontas told her brothers she was grieved that her father had been unwilling to give up his weapons to ransom her and that she liked the English so much that she planned to marry and stay with them.

To Dale's surprise, Powhatan gave permission for the marriage, but he did not attend the ceremony, held in Jamestown on April 5, 1614. He gave his daughter a necklace of freshwater pearls; her uncle gave her away.

The newlyweds lived on a plantation on the James River between Henrico and Jamestown. The land was a gift from Powhatan. They called their plantation Varina for a variety of Spanish tobacco Rolfe grew.

After his daughter's marriage, Powhatan made peace with the English that lasted the remainder of his lifetime.

In 1615 Pocahontas and John Rolfe had a son they named Thomas. In appreciation of all the good Pocahontas had done for the colony, the Virginia Company—a group of investors who financed colonization in Virginia—voted to give her and her son an annual stipend. The only person not pleased with this was King James, who declared that Rolfe had committed treason by marrying the daughter of a pagan king.

The following year the Virginia Company invited the Rolfes to visit England as a way to attract attention—and thus more settlers—to Virginia.

On June 12, 1616, the Rolfes arrived in England, accompanied by a group of Pocahontas's relatives. Her sister's husband, Tomocomo, had been instructed by Powhatan to cut a notch in a stick for every Englishman he saw. The poor man soon gave up, seeing the multitudes in England. John Smith wrote Queen Anne, persuading her to receive Pocahontas in gratitude for all the princess had done for Virginia. Pocahontas was also entertained by the Bishop of London, and twice had her portrait painted. The more familiar portrait shows her wearing an elaborate red and black Elizabethan costume and hat. Her coat is trimmed in gold, and lace surrounds her very fair face and hand. In the second she wears a simple skirt and embroidered blouse, her skin is tawny, and her features are more like those of a Native American. She is sitting with her arm around her son Thomas.

Everywhere the Rolfes went, Pocahontas was welcomed, feted, and praised. When Pocahontas began to suffer respiratory problems, the Rolfes left London for Brentford Inn. Here John Smith came for a very emotional visit. The two had not met for eight years, and Pocahontas had thought her captain dead. She scolded him for not sending her some word. She was now a stranger in his land as he had once been in hers, but the bonds forged years before had made them countrymen and kinsmen.

The Rolfes next visited John's family home, Heacham, so his family could meet Rolfe's wife and son. After a few weeks the Rolfes returned to the tiring London social scene and prepared to sail for Virginia. Pocahontas wanted to stay in England, despite the damp climate that kept her coughing, but Rolfe longed to be back in Virginia.

At Gravesend, while waiting for their departure to Virginia, in March 1617, Pocahontas became gravely ill and died. The cause may have been tuberculosis or smallpox. She was buried on the day of her death in the churchyard of St. George's Parish, far from her native land. She was only twenty or twenty-one years old.

The Jamestown colony might have failed without the aid of Pocahontas. Her marriage to an Englishman brought seven years of peace with the Powhatan tribe. She played a role in the future of Virginia as well, for through her son Thomas she became the ancestor of numerous descendants, including a First Lady of the United States.

MARTHA
WASHINGTON
1731–1802

The First First Lady

*I*t was a lovely spring day in 1757 at Poplar Grove Plantation in New Kent County, Virginia. The guests, including recently widowed Martha Dandridge Custis, were just sitting down for lunch when the host, Richard Chamberlayne, entered with a tall man in the uniform of the Colonial Army.

Chamberlayne introduced the new arrival: "Colonel George Washington, who is on his way to Williamsburg for a meeting with Governor Dinwiddie. I have persuaded him to pause in his journey for refreshment with us."

Washington, saying that he must be on his way soon after lunch, took a seat at the dining table next to Martha Custis, and the two chatted of friends, family, and events in Virginia. He expressed his respect for her deceased husband and described the work he was doing at his plantation, Mount Vernon, in northern Virginia. She listened with interest to his description of military expeditions on the frontier and of his mission to Governor Dinwiddie.

The two continued their conversation after lunch ended, delaying Washington's departure for Williamsburg. By the time he left the following day, he had asked if on his return he might call

Martha Washington

on Mrs. Custis at her plantation, the White House, just across the Pamunkey River. Martha agreed, knowing a significant chapter in her life was beginning.

Martha was born on June 21, 1731, to Colonel John Dandridge and his wife, Frances, at Chestnut Grove, their plantation in New Kent County, Virginia. The Dandridge family was large: Martha, John, William, Bartholomew, Nancy, and Frances. Martha was taught to sew, play the spinet, and dance the minuet, suitable accomplishments for a young girl of the 1700s. She disliked math and spelling, and throughout her life was a poor speller. More importantly, she learned to cook and to manage a household. Servants would do the work, but as the future mistress of a plantation, she had to know how to supervise. Martha believed her career would be as a wife and mother.

At age fifteen Martha was presented at the Governor's Ball in Williamsburg, where she attracted the attention of many suitors, including Daniel Parke Custis. The thirty-year-old was one of the wealthiest young men in Virginia, making him quite a "catch" for Martha despite the difference in their ages. Such marriages were not uncommon in Virginia. However, Daniel's father intended him to marry a cousin, Evelyn Byrd, even though Evelyn was in love with someone else. Eventually the elder Mr. Custis accepted Martha, and she and Daniel were married in June 1749, when Martha was eighteen.

Daniel Custis was a member of the King's Council, the governing body of the time. The couple led an active social life, dividing their time between White House plantation and Six Chimney House in Williamsburg when the Assembly was in session. Soon Martha and Daniel had two children, Daniel and Frances. Life was good for them.

Then grief and joy came in quick succession. In 1752 their son Daniel died. The following year they had another son, John

Parke Custis V, called Jacky. In 1755 baby Frances died, and so did Martha's beloved father. Two months later, Martha gave birth to another daughter, Martha Parke Custis, called Patsy.

The final tragedy for Martha was Daniel's illness and death. He grew thin and weak and was unable to make the journey from the plantation to Williamsburg to attend King's Council meetings. He died in August 1757. After eight years of marriage, twenty-six-year old Martha was a widow with two small children. Daniel's will had made her executor of his estate and one of the wealthiest women in Virginia.

After his meeting with Martha Custis at the Chamberlayne home in 1757, George Washington concluded his business in Williamsburg and visited her at White House. On this visit, only the second time the two had ever seen each other, he asked Martha to marry him and she agreed. But he first had to return to military duty on the frontier. While he was away, he was elected to the House of Burgesses from Frederick County, where he owned property. Then word came from the Ohio Territory that the French had given up Fort Duquesne to the English and Washington would soon be back in Williamsburg. Excitedly, Martha planned a wedding and looked forward to George's return.

He wrote ahead to Martha: ". . . I embrace the opportunity to send a few words to one whose life is inseparable from mine. Since that happy hour when we made our pledges to each other my thoughts have been continually going to you as to another self."

Their wedding, on January 6, 1759, was a brilliant social event, attended by prominent Virginians and the new governor, Francis Fauquier. The groom wore a blue suit, the jacket lined with scarlet, and gold knee buckles. The bride's dress was white silk shot with silver. Pearls were entwined in her hair and around her neck, and her satin slippers were clasped with diamond buckles.

As Martha's husband, George was legally entitled to a third of her estate and was entrusted with the care of Martha's two remaining children, Jacky and Patsy. He managed the estates so well that by the time Jacky reached legal age, their value had doubled.

The Washingtons moved to Mount Vernon, the estate in Fairfax County that George had inherited from his brother Lawrence. They took along Martha's children and servants, and wagonloads of furnishings. Soon Martha was managing the Mount Vernon household, getting up early to see to breakfast preparations, tending the sick, and making guests feel welcome. George wanted her to continue living in the style and comfort she was used to and to have time to enjoy being with him and the children. He hired a steward to take over many household duties and ordered a handsome new coach as well as fashionable clothes from London. He wanted only the best for her, and she wanted to make a comfortable home for him.

The Washingtons' nearest neighbors were George William Fairfax and his wife, Sally. Washington had been friends with Fairfax and his family for years, and gossip had spread that he felt more than friendship for Sally. Martha knew she could never compete in looks with the tall, beautiful Sally, nor could she carry on sophisticated conversation as Sally did. Still, jealousy would serve no purpose. George had chosen her as a wife, and Sally was married to his friend. Determined to ignore the gossip, Martha befriended Sally.

Years passed happily at Mount Vernon. George enjoyed the life of a country squire, and Martha enjoyed being his wife and the mistress of a busy, profitable plantation. So many visitors came to the place that Washington once joked that they were running a fine tavern. In 1773, however, their lives were changed by events beyond their plantation.

George and other soldiers had not been given the land promised them for fighting in the French and Indian War, which had ended a decade earlier. Washington was in Williamsburg petitioning Governor John Murray, the Earl of Dunmore, for payment when Martha's sixteen-year-old daughter Patsy, always frail, became sick. Martha sent George an urgent message, and he arrived back at Mount Vernon shortly before Patsy's death.

Despite her grief, Martha forced herself to smile and be strong for George, who was facing political and financial problems. Britain had imposed new taxes, and the colonials responded by boycotting British products. Governor Dunmore, as John Murray was called, dismissed the House of Burgesses, sending Washington and other delegates home. A split with the mother country seemed inevitable, and everyone chose sides. George and Sally Fairfax, who sided with the king in the dispute, left Belvoir Plantation for England. Fairfax asked Washington to look after his plantation until his return, but the manor house burned and the Washingtons never saw their neighbors again.

Martha's son, Jacky Custis, was a disappointment to her and to George. He never settled down to serious work, instead spending his time idly. At eighteen he fell in love with Eleanor Calvert, daughter of a distinguished Maryland family, and wanted to marry her immediately. Washington sent him to King's College in New York (now Columbia University), hoping that Jacky would get over Eleanor and apply himself to his studies. But Jacky idled away more time and persisted in his wish to marry his teenage love. Finally, Washington relented and gave permission for the marriage.

In 1774 Martha was left at Mount Vernon when George went to Philadelphia to attend the first Continental Congress, an attempt to unite the colonies against England. He returned to Mount Vernon for the winter of 1775.

In April of that year, loyalist Governor Dunmore seized Virginia's supply of ammunition from Williamsburg, and in Massachusetts, citizen militia and British soldiers shot at each other at Lexington and Concord. War had begun. Washington again left Mount Vernon for the Continental Congress meeting in Philadelphia. Martha was left alone in Virginia once more, but it would not be for long, she thought. The Congress would end and George would return home. Then a letter came from him saying he had been made Commander of the American Army and was on his way to Boston to take charge of the troops. This time they would be separated by an even greater distance.

Months passed, during which all Martha could do to help George was write warm, cheerful letters. He urged her to join him in winter quarters in Cambridge, Massachusetts, but she had never been outside Virginia and felt trepidation at such a long trip.

Then a rumor spread that she, the general's wife, was a Tory, sympathetic to England! The only way she knew to scotch the rumor was to go to George, to show her support of America's army.

Martha packed their valuables away in storage, lest Governor Dunmore make good on his threat to sail up the Potomac and shell Washington's plantation to punish the traitorous general. She left Mount Vernon in the charge of George's cousin, Lund Washington, and gathered all the food, wine, and warm clothing she could fit into her carriage. Accompanied by Jacky and Eleanor, Martha set out for Massachusetts.

In every city they passed through, they were met by an honor guard of Continental Army troops to escort them. The Washington coach, with four white horses, attracted attention in the countryside too, and all along the route, people waved to the general's lady.

Finally, after passing through Pennsylvania and New York, they arrived at Washington's headquarters just before Christmas. George had not wanted Martha to endure the privations his army was suffering, but he was overjoyed to see her. Martha set about doing what she knew best: She cooked, mended, tended the sick, and distributed food and cheer. Other officers' wives came to call, dressed in their finery. They found Martha Washington in home-spun, wearing an apron and knitting a pair of socks for George.

She soon organized the wives into a working team, doing whatever they could to make life a little better for the men of the Continental Army.

When summer came and the army moved into position for the next campaign against the British, Martha left, returning to Mount Vernon.

For the next six years of war, Martha spent the winter months with George wherever the Army was, and her summers at their plantation, seeing to the harvesting and preserving of food. In those eight years, Jacky and Eleanor became the parents of four children, Martha's grandchildren. Jacky had never gone to fight, as most men his age had done, and Martha knew this troubled George. Other young men Jacky's age were fighting and dying, while he continued living in safety and luxury.

In the late summer of 1781, Washington returned to Mount Vernon for the first time in six years, but only briefly. He was on his way to Yorktown, accompanied by the French general Comte de Rochambeau and the young Marquis de Lafayette. When they left the following day, Jacky went along. He had finally decided to join his stepfather in the fight for freedom.

In October General Lord Charles Cornwallis surrendered at Yorktown, and soon word came to Mount Vernon that Jacky was desperately ill of trench fever. Martha and Eleanor made the four-day journey to his bedside at a plantation near Williamsburg shortly before he died.

Martha and George adopted Jacky's two younger children: Eleanor, called Nelly, who was two, and George Washington Parke Custis, a baby of six months. Jacky's widow, Eleanor, soon remarried.

Peace came to America, and George and Martha Washington enjoyed being together at last at Mount Vernon, again entertaining friends and family, including Lafayette, who came back to America to visit. Martha's happiness was marred only by the deaths in 1785 of her mother and her brother Bart.

George Washington enjoyed the life of a country squire, riding about his estate, supervising his gristmill, grafting and planting trees, inspecting livestock and horses, and doing a thousand other tasks necessary for running a plantation, but he had financial worries. Mount Vernon, left in the charge of others during the war, had produced little during the time he had been away, and he had been paid nothing for his eight years of service in the Army. He had, in fact, furnished his own uniforms, horses, and food. By appealing to Congress and to the Virginia government, Washington was finally able to get his soldiers compensated, mostly with western land.

America itself was having problems. Visitors to Mount Vernon complained of a lack of cooperation among the thirteen states, each of which had its own money and its own tariffs on goods from the other states.

Washington suggested a meeting of delegates from states bordering on the Chesapeake Bay, to discuss trade and shipping. He attended the meeting at Annapolis to represent Virginia. The delegates decided that the problems extended beyond their boundaries. All the states should meet and form a stronger union, or else, the freedom they had fought for might be lost to some stronger nation. Washington wanted to retire from public life, but he was the first Virginian nominated to attend the convention.

In Philadelphia, George was chosen to preside at the convention that wrote what became the U. S. Constitution. Afterward, he returned to Mount Vernon to await the states' decisions on whether to ratify the Constitution.

In the spring of 1789, word came that the first congress had met and had unanimously chosen George Washington the first president of the United States. Martha knew it meant four more years away from Mount Vernon, from her family, and from Virginia, four years in New York among strangers. Still, George was obviously the best choice to lead the new nation, and her job was to help him. Once again the family packed for a journey northward.

Both Martha and George saw the importance of their undertaking. The new nation would need to be peaceful and unified if it were to succeed. There must be no dissension that would rip apart the frail union. As the president and his lady, they would be watched, their actions studied, criticized, and perhaps copied by future presidents and their wives.

George's role was spelled out in the Constitution, but what was Martha's? As she saw it, her job as the president's wife was the job she had taken on so many years ago as the wife of young George Washington: She must make a comfortable, serene home for him so that he could go out and handle the nation's business. She must not listen to gossip or repeat it. She must be able to entertain heads of state, for now her husband was himself a head of state, and she must also treat kindly those more lowly born, for this was America.

Most of all, no matter how much she longed for the solitude of Mount Vernon, she must never let her discontent show, or bother George with such petty matters.

Martha was called the President's Lady or Lady Washington, and because she was the first to be in that position, her title and consequently that of those who followed became First Lady.

The Washingtons had always been early risers, and they continued to be. On one occasion, when Rembrandt Peale was commissioned to paint Martha's portrait as a companion to his famous portrait of George, the time for the first sitting was set at seven in the morning. Peale arrived on time, but thought it was too early to disturb Mrs. Washington, so he took a walk. Returning, he knocked, was admitted and told by Mrs. Washington that he was late. When he explained his reasoning, she said that she had already had devotions, taught Nelly a music lesson, and read the newspaper.

The Washingtons also went to bed early. Martha began a pattern of Friday evening receptions, during which she and George would mingle with their guests, free of the ceremony such receptions usually entailed. She wanted people to feel at ease when talking with the president. She was adamant, however, that George should get enough rest. At a few minutes before nine, she would tell her guests that the president always retired at nine and that she usually went a few minutes before he did. The guests had no choice but to say a quick good-night.

In 1792, to Martha's dismay, the electors chose her husband for another four-year term as president. There were some who wanted him to be president for life, or even king. George accepted the nomination, but decided that two terms were more than enough. Europeans were amazed when at the end of his term he willingly, happily, gave up power and went home to Mount Vernon.

The Washingtons had only three more years together at Mount Vernon. On December 12, 1799, George rode out as usual to oversee his plantation, and he returned to the house with a sore throat. Over the next few days it grew worse, and doctors were summoned. Following the crude medical practices of the time, they applied mustard plasters to his throat and chest and bled him, taking out nine pints over two days. At one point, Martha protested further bleeding, but George was willing, and the practice continued. Not surprisingly, he grew worse. He asked Martha to stay by his side and sent for his will to be reviewed. George died late in the evening of December 14, at age sixty-seven.

Martha was bereft and believed that she would soon join him. When she sensed her own end approaching, she called Nelly and George Washington Custis to her bedside. She didn't live to see how well they turned out. Nelly married Washington's favorite nephew, Fielding Lewis. Washington Custis became a successful writer and painter.

Martha Dandridge Custis Washington died on May 22, 1802, and is buried beside her beloved George at Mount Vernon.

ELIZABETH HENRY RUSSELL
1749–1825

Madame Russell

$\mathscr{E}$lizabeth Henry Campbell Russell was the sister of one of the most famous men in Virginia and the wife of two Revolutionary War generals, yet it is for her religious work in the mountains of western Virginia that she is best known.

Elizabeth was the sister of Patrick Henry, known in Virginia history as the orator who challenged the royal governor and King George III, calling for revolution with the phrase "Give me liberty or give me death!"

The Henrys lived in Hanover County, and Elizabeth—or Betsy, as she was sometimes called—grew up in a privileged environment. The Henrys' plantation home was spacious enough to accommodate the growing family, and servants did the hard labor. This was poor preparation for the life Betsy was to lead on the frontier during wartime.

In 1775 Betsy was living in Williamsburg, acting as hostess for her widowed brother Patrick, entertaining members of the House of Burgesses, prominent landowners, and military officers who came to call. Times were tense. Taxes imposed by the British government on lead, paper, paint, and tea, and the expensive stamps

"Madame" Elizabeth Henry Russell

required on all legal documents angered the Virginians. Governor John Murray, the Earl of Dunmore, expecting trouble from the local militia, removed the weapons and gunpowder from the colony's arsenal, further angering the public. Patrick Henry called for troops to defend the colony against its royal governor.

One of those who answered Henry's call to arms was thirty-three-year-old Colonel William Campbell, who lived in Western Virginia with his mother and four sisters at a place called Aspenvale, in what is now Washington County. He had inherited from his father a tract of land in western Virginia that included a salt lick, a place where salt oozed from the ground and could be harvested and sold. When Henry called for troops, Campbell marched with his riflemen 400 miles to Williamsburg.

Campbell met twenty-six-year-old Betsy Henry, and the two fell in love. It was considered a good match for them both. Betsy was older than most unmarried Virginia girls, but she came from a politically powerful family. Campbell was not only handsome, but eligible because of his property, and he too was older than many men at a first marriage.

Campbell and the rest of Henry's troops didn't need to fight—this time. Governor Dunmore agreed to pay for the powder he'd taken, and a military confrontation was avoided. But Virginia's militia stayed ready.

On April 21, 1776, less than a year after their meeting, Elizabeth Henry became William Campbell's wife in a quiet family ceremony. A few days later, William was back on military duty, and Elizabeth went to stay with her parents. The newlyweds wrote each other affectionate, newsy letters. In one, William mentioned requesting that soldiers be stationed near his home in western Virginia to protect against Indian attacks, but his request was denied. Elizabeth may have been a bit frightened at the thought of living with the possibility of attack, but she loved her husband and would gladly go wherever he chose to live.

Finally, late in 1776, the couple could be together. They made the weeks-long journey to southwest Virginia, to Campbell's Aspenvale, where Elizabeth faced the privations and dangers of life on the frontier. She took along three servants, but there was much menial work to be done to produce things as simple as soap, which in eastern Virginia could be purchased from abroad. Aspenvale was a simple log house, different from the mansions of Williamsburg. Neighbors were far away, and elaborate dinners and balls had been left behind at the capital.

On January 1, 1777, Campbell helped organize Washington County, Virginia. He was not only a magistrate but a military commander, responsible for the order and safety of his district. Completely American, he hated Tories, or British sympathizers. One day a Tory called while he was out, asking Elizabeth to persuade her husband to ease off in his harsh treatment of his Tory neighbors. Campbell came in, saw the man, and reached for his sword to kill him. Elizabeth grabbed her husband's upraised arm so that the sword cut into the door frame instead of the visitor, who fled. When he'd had time to cool down, Campbell thanked his wife for intervening. The Tory should be hanged, he said, not cut down within his home.

Soon a daughter, Sarah Buchanan Campbell, and a son, Charles Henry Campbell, were born to Elizabeth and William, then came war with England. Campbell again answered the call of Virginia and marched away, leaving Elizabeth to run the farm and look after the family.

Campbell was a superb military man. Because of his heroism in the Battle of King's Mountain and Guilford Courthouse in 1780, he was promoted to brigadier general and returned home.

His stay was brief. In August 1781 he was again called to military duty. British General Lord Cornwallis had arrived in Virginia from the Carolinas, and General George Washington hoped to defeat him with the help of the French. All troops were needed. General Campbell marched away from Elizabeth for the last time. In Williamsburg he caught a fever—perhaps typhoid—and was taken to the home of Colonel John Symes, Elizabeth's half brother, where he died a few days later, just months before the Americans defeated Cornwallis and won their freedom from England.

Under the terms of his will, General Campbell left the salt lick property to his daughter, Sarah, and granted Elizabeth a life interest in Aspenvale.

The Campbells' son had not been born when the will was written, so no bequest was made to him, but the State of Virginia granted him 5,000 acres of land in gratitude for his father's military service. Young Charles Henry Campbell's uncle, Arthur Campbell, as executor, chose land next to the salt lick for him, and patented additional land for both Charles and Sarah. After Charles died in childhood, his land passed to his sister, who thus became a very wealthy young girl.

In 1781, the year William Campbell died, General William Russell, who owned land near Castlewood on the Clinch River, arrived in the Washington County area. Recognizing the importance of salt production, he bought additional land near the salt lick.

In 1776 Russell had been a member of the House of Burgesses from Fincastle County. He and Elizabeth might have met in passing in Williamsburg, but at the time she would have paid him no attention, for her heart belonged to William Campbell. General Russell, a widower, had children from his first marriage to Tabitha Adams, daughter of Massachusetts patriot Samuel Adams. Soon Russell and the widowed Elizabeth became friends, and in 1783 they married. They continued to live at Aspenvale for five years.

Over the next ten years, the Russells had four children: two daughters, Elizabeth and Jane, and two sons who died in infancy. General Russell was a stern man and a strict disciplinarian who often angered Elizabeth's daughter Sarah. Sarah perhaps felt an allegiance to her father, who was honored by many Virginians, resenting any man who might try to take her father's place. Elizabeth felt torn between her young children, her older daughter, and her husband.

The antagonism between Sarah Campbell and her stepfather grew as Russell attempted to manage Sarah's property. Arthur Campbell objected to Russell's decisions, and finally a court assigned Sarah a guardian, Thomas Madison, who had married Elizabeth's sister, Susanna Henry. Sarah went to live with the Madisons. Elizabeth had now lost her first husband and her sons to death and her daughter to a court decision.

In 1788 General Russell moved his family away from Aspenvale to a house he'd had built on the edge of the salt lick in what is now Saltville in Smythe County. He dug brine wells and began producing salt. Because of the Russells' wealth and prominence, people began to refer to Elizabeth as Madame Russell.

In the late spring of 1788, soon after the Russells moved to the salt lick, the Methodist Church fathers held a conference in the Holston River area. The presiding bishop, Francis Asbury, who was to conduct the conference, was detained elsewhere for a week, apparently because of the threat of Indian attack along his route from Rutherford Courthouse, North Carolina. In the meantime Reverend Thomas Ware held a preaching service a few miles from the Russells' home.

Elizabeth and her family had belonged to the Church of England. After the American Revolution, the Church of England became the Episcopal Church of North America, using the same buildings and conducting services in the same way. Elizabeth was thus an Episcopalian. She took Holy Communion as often as possible on the frontier, read the Bible, and was kind and helpful to her neighbors.

Some considered William Russell "a proud opposer of godliness." Although neither Elizabeth nor William was Methodist, they attended Ware's service, and Elizabeth was moved by the sermon. Afterward, she approached Ware and told him that although she had always considered herself a Christian, she realized she was the "veriest of sinners." She asked the ministers to come to her house and pray for her.

The group arrived and spent the afternoon in prayer, but Elizabeth still felt that she had not been saved. After the ministers left, General Russell read the Bible aloud to her and continued praying, at her request. By evening, when the ministers returned, Elizabeth proclaimed that she had been forgiven and saved. Now General Russell began to pray and weep, demanding prayer on his own behalf, since his wife had been blessed and he had not. By the time Bishop Asbury arrived, the Methodist Church could claim two distinguished converts.

Bishop Asbury noted in his diary that he stayed with the Russells and was thankful to have time to be alone in prayer. It was customary then for circuit-riding ministers to stay with whomever was willing to put them up for the night. Often they shared not only a room but a bed with family members and had scant food. Not so at the Russells', where the bishop had privacy and comfort. The bishop visited the area again in 1790 and noted that he had a good prayer meeting at the Russells' home.

In 1792 William Russell's health deteriorated. He had been elected to the Virginia legislature and intended to go to Richmond for the opening session in January 1793, stopping in Shenandoah County for a short visit with his son Robert. When he prepared to leave on December 15, however, he was so feeble that Elizabeth decided to take their two daughters and accompany him. Russell's older daughter and her husband also went along.

The party stopped off for a short visit with Thomas and Susanna Madison in Botetourt County and didn't arrive at Robert

Russell's home until January 1. William Russell, who had caught a cold on the winter journey, developed influenza and died on January 14. The family returned with his body to Saltville, and William was buried in his beloved southwest Virginia.

Although she had not married until she was twenty-seven, by the age of forty-four Elizabeth was twice widowed. She was named executrix of Russell's estate and soon reached a settlement with his adult children. In return for a small sum to support herself and her daughters, Elizabeth and Jane, then seven and five years old, she relinquished her rights to any of William's property, but protected that of the girls.

In May, Bishop Asbury again visited the Russell home, which he now called "Sister Russell's." He noted that he missed the general, who he felt sure was already "in Abraham's bosom." The bishop visited again in 1797, 1801, and 1802. On the 1802 visit he was in poor health and believed that it was to be his last trip there. He wondered what would become of the Methodist flock when Sister Russell had gone. He lived to make one more visit to the Holston area, in 1806, and noted that he found Widow Russell "as happy and cheerful as ever."

Sarah Campbell, Elizabeth's daughter, was sent away for schooling and in 1793, at the age of fifteen, she married the wealthy and distinguished General Francis Preston. Educated in law at the College of William and Mary, Preston was friends with Thomas Jefferson, James Madison, and James Monroe, and was repeatedly elected to the Virginia legislature.

The couple moved to Abingdon, and Francis was soon elected to the U.S. Congress from the Montgomery District of Virginia. He and Sarah then moved to Philadelphia, where in 1794 their first son, William Campbell Preston, was born. The Prestons renewed their acquaintance with Dolley Payne Todd, Elizabeth Russell's cousin, who later became Mrs. James Madison.

After her conversion to Methodism, Elizabeth began to look seriously at her life and her property. She had given up most of the salt lick property soon after General Russell's death, and after Sarah's marriage she transferred her rights to the Campbell estate to her daughter.

Elizabeth lived simply and never kept a carriage, preferring to ride about on horseback, which some of her neighbors considered scandalous. Although she had divested herself of most worldly goods, Elizabeth still owned slaves, and she came to see that owning another human was morally wrong. Her neighbors and other family members were horrified to learn that she planned to set her slaves free. A number of Virginians freed slaves in their wills, but very few were willing to give up the slaves' labor during their own lifetime.

Elizabeth owned outright the three slaves she had brought with her from Hanover County, and these she set free. William Campbell had promised to free his servant, John Brawdy, when he returned from Yorktown, but had not lived to do so. Elizabeth felt she was carrying out General Campbell's wishes the best she could when she freed Brawdy for the rest of her life, and providing him a home near the salt lick. But because she only had a life interest in Campbell's property, on her death Brawdy again became a slave.

In the deed that freed her slaves in January 1795, Elizabeth declared that "aided by a just and good God, it is both sinful and unjust" to own slaves because they were "by nature equally free with myself."

Madame Russell's second family grew up. Her daughter Elizabeth married Francis Smith in January 1804, but she died suddenly later in the year. Her share of the Russell property went to her sister Jane, who married Dr. William Patton Thompson, a wealthy Abingdon man. Thompson owned nearly 10,000 acres of land and a home called Town House; from here one supposedly could see all the way to Abingdon, 18 miles away.

Elizabeth reconciled with her daughter Sarah, and after the Prestons returned to Virginia from Philadelphia, they lived in the house built by Thomas and Susanna Madison, across the lake from Madame Russell's house.

In 1808, when James Madison was nominated for the presidency, he and his wife Dolley visited Elizabeth and the Prestons. Madison commented on the wonderful hospitality he received there, and on Elizabeth's commanding voice. Anyone who visited her was welcomed in and urged to pray with her. Placing her hand on his head, Elizabeth pressed the future president down to a kneeling position so that he might pray with her.

Elizabeth's oldest grandson, William Campbell Preston, had made a trip to Europe, and when the family welcomed him home, Elizabeth led the group in a prayer of thanks for his return, concluding with gratitude that God had shielded him from the wiles of foreign women and brought him back unencumbered by a frivolous wife.

In 1812 the Prestons moved into Abingdon and built a house, which burned soon after it was completed. They moved into another house nearby and urged Elizabeth to move into town with them. Reluctantly she agreed, and asked their son William to find a house for her. He told her he'd found one on an adjoining lot, on the backstreet behind the Prestons. Indignant, she said she wouldn't live on a backstreet! It was insulting to suggest it. Moreover, she preferred the country to Abingdon, which she considered an impious and sinful town.

She went instead to live near her daughter Jane and Jane's husband, Dr. Thompson, at Sulphur Springs, now Chilhowie. The log house they provided for Elizabeth was a story and a half tall, simple and barnlike. One room on the lower floor was Elizabeth's bedroom and parlor. Beside it was a much larger room that had a pulpit and seats enough for a church congregation. Whenever a visiting minister came to the area, she would gather friends and neighbors and insist that he preach a service.

Guests were always welcome and were fed well. Women stayed in one room while men stayed in a separate building in the yard. For the destitute she provided new clothing and even a horse to ride on to the next settlement. Her needs were simple, so she used her resources to care for others.

In 1824 a Methodist church was built in Saltville near the site of the Russell home. It was named Elizabeth Church in her honor.

In the winter of 1825 Madame Russell had a serious fall and was bedridden for the next five weeks. She died on March 18, 1825, at the age of seventy-six, and was buried at Aspenvale.

In 1898 a new church was begun a few feet from the Russell home and was named Madame Russell Memorial United Methodist Church. One of its stained glass windows holds the images of Bishop Francis Asbury and Elizabeth Henry Campbell Russell. Her reconstructed home stands beside the church and is simply furnished, much as it was when she lived there.

Emory and Henry College nearby was not named for Patrick Henry as many suppose, but for Elizabeth Henry, known to residents of Southwest Virginia as Madame Russell.

Dolley Madison
1768–1849

America's Hostess

*B*y late August, 1814, it was clear that British troops were headed for America's capital, Washington, D.C. President Madison ordered that American government archives be sent to Virginia for safekeeping on August 23, and he urged his wife, Dolley, to leave immediately. But she refused to leave until she knew he too would be safe.

On the morning of the 24th, Madison rode out into Maryland to see the military situation for himself, and Dolley began packing. Later that afternoon, the boom of a cannon sounded in the distance, and then Dolley heard artillery shells, much closer. Running outside, she commandeered a wagon and ordered her small carriage to be brought to the door of the White House. With the reluctant help of some bystanders, the First Lady loaded the presidential papers into the wagon, along with the White House draperies, china, silver, and some books.

A friend, Matilda Love, arrived and told Dolley she could wait no longer to leave. Ignoring the Madisons' own belongings, Dolley carried out portraits of former presidents John Adams and Thomas Jefferson. The portrait of George Washington was too big

Dolley Madison

to carry, so she cut the famous painting from its frame and put it into her own carriage.

Dolley and Matilda left Washington, with Dolley driving the carriage and a soldier driving the wagon. By nightfall they—and America's treasures—were safe at a farm in Virginia.

When she was a child, few would have predicted that Dolley would become a heroine in wartime or that she would be America's First Lady and the most popular Washington hostess for two decades.

One of Virginia's most famous women, Dolley Payne was born in North Carolina, where her parents, both aristocratic Virginians, were living temporarily. There were already two sons in the family when Dolley was born in 1768. The Paynes would eventually have four more daughters and two more sons. Dolley's name was Dorothea, but for most of her life she was known as Dolley, spelled Dolly by some.

The Payne family moved back to Virginia, and when Dolley was eleven her father bought Scotchtown, a huge frame house owned by their cousin, Patrick Henry. James Madison visited there, as well as two other future presidents: Thomas Jefferson and James Monroe. At the time of his visit, Madison did not have any romantic interest in Dolley. She was a tomboy riding about the plantation on her pony and challenging boys to footraces when the twenty-eight-year-old Madison was a member of Virginia's legislature, involved in planning the kind of government the new nation called America would have.

Because Dolley's parents were Quakers, she had a strict upbringing with few luxuries. At the end of the Revolutionary War, the Paynes, who opposed slavery but owned slaves, decided to free them and move to Philadelphia. Virginia law required that owners who freed slaves provide for them and move them out of the state. This was a financial burden that left little for the Paynes to live on in Philadelphia. Several of the freed slaves went along as house servants and were thereafter paid wages.

Philadelphia was the largest city in America, a bustling, prosperous place full of all kinds of people, not just Quakers. It was exciting, but the Payne family's standard of living dropped. John Payne invested in western lands and in a starch business that failed, and the family, used to an acre of gardens and hundreds of acres of plantation, now had to live in a small house.

Dolley was enrolled in a Quaker school, along with her sisters and brothers, but she discovered that the tutoring she'd had in Virginia had left her far behind others her age, and she dropped out at sixteen. She was already attracting attention for her beauty—a plump figure, dark curly hair, and long-lashed dark eyes—and she planned to marry and stay near her parents. Her mother's health was poor from bearing so many children, and the house servant they'd brought from Virginia died, so Dolley spent her days cooking and sewing.

When the Constitutional Convention met in Philadelphia in 1787, Dolley was nineteen. Members of the Virginia delegation, including George Washington and James Madison, visited the Paynes, but still there was no romance between James and Dolley. He was totally involved in writing the Constitution, and she may have found him austere and aloof.

In 1789 the Constitution was ratified and the nation's capital was moved from New York to Philadelphia. The following year, James Madison was elected to the House of Representatives.

Dolley's father had borrowed money after his starch business failed. When he couldn't repay the debt, he was banished by the Quakers. The family was destitute. Two sons left for Virginia to farm, and Mrs. Payne took in boarders. Dolley, at twenty-one, decided to marry John Todd, who, despite being overweight and humorless, was nevertheless very "eligible." A twenty-five-year-old

Quaker lawyer, Todd had a thriving business and already owned a house. He and Dolley were married in January 1790; in less than a year they were the proud parents of a son, Payne Todd. Dolley spoiled him outrageously and never learned to tell him no.

Dolley's life changed drastically over the next few years. Her sister Lucy married George Washington's favorite nephew and went to live in Jefferson County, Virginia (now West Virginia). Her father, John Payne, died in 1792. On July 4, 1793, Dolley gave birth to her second son, in the midst of a yellow fever epidemic. Dolley insisted on staying in the city with her husband and children, but when his parents were stricken, Dolley agreed to leave. John stayed on to care for his parents, who both died. Then John himself died, as did Dolley's baby son. Although Dolley also contracted yellow fever, she recovered.

The twenty-four-year-old widow had no need to remarry. She owned her house outright, and Todd had left her $10,000 in cash, although it took months of negotiations and finally the threat of lawsuits before the other Todd heirs agreed to settle with her.

James Madison then took an interest in Dolley, as did other suitors. One of these was Aaron Burr, a married man whom Dolley sent packing. Madison made his intentions clear, sending word that he would call on her, always with chaperones.

Madison, whose friends considered him a confirmed bachelor, had fallen in love, and he was determined to win Dolley's heart. When she announced plans to visit her sister, Lucy Washington, in Virginia, Madison arranged everything: horses, carriages, and inns along the way. Then he rode beside the carriage and played with her son, Payne. Madison returned to his home, Montpelier, and sent frequent letters to Dolley at Harewood, her sister's home. Finally, Dolley gave in to Madison's courtship and married him in September 1794. She had been a widow less than a year.

When the Madisons returned to Philadelphia after their

honeymoon, their happiness was obvious to everyone. In a time when many marriages were often just business arrangements, the Madisons were deeply in love.

Soon after their return, Dolley was expelled from the Society of Friends for marrying a non-Quaker. Hurt, she said that in her heart she would always share the beliefs of Quakers. At the same time, however, she was glad to be released from some of the restrictions of the Society. Now she could wear bright clothes cut in the latest style and lead an active social life.

Madison proudly indulged her, on one occasion ordering her twenty pairs of shoes at once. He was also a good stepfather to her son, who was soon calling Madison "Papa."

When Congress adjourned in 1795, Madison took Dolley to Montpelier, his twenty-nine-room mansion in Orange County, Virginia. Dolley loved the house and got along well with his parents, who lived at the mansion. As eldest son, James would inherit Montpelier, and his mother was delighted that he had married. Nelly Madison and Dolley got along so well that after her husband's death, Nelly continued to live with James and Dolley instead of going to live with one of her daughters, as was more customary. The younger Madisons built her a four-room apartment and added wings and columned porticoes to the already huge house.

After six weeks at Montpelier, the Madisons returned to Philadelphia, where Dolley created a sensation by wearing the latest Paris fashions, cut low on the bosom, with a high waist and thin, draped skirts. She also refused to wear powdered wigs, preferring her own hair, elaborately styled.

In 1796 John Adams, a Federalist, was elected president, and Thomas Jefferson, a Republican, became vice president. The Madisons left Philadelphia for Montpelier, and James Madison announced his intention to retire from politics. He disliked the Federalists' policy of increasing the central government's power at the expense of the states. He would not run for office again, he said, but intended to become a country squire, happy with his wife and family about him.

The Madisons frequently entertained at Montpelier, made two lengthy visits to the Jeffersons at Monticello, and visited with James and Elizabeth Monroe, who had built a house nearby. Although disappointed that they never had children of their own, James and Dolley had son Payne and her sister Anna living with them, as well as James's mother and Nelly Conway Madison, the daughter of James's late brother.

Madison reentered politics when Patrick Henry, a Federalist, announced that he was running for the Virginia legislature. With Dolley at his side, Madison ran as a delegate from Orange County and won. This was the first time a candidate's wife had campaigned politically in Virginia.

The Madisons' future changed again in 1800, when Thomas Jefferson won the presidency after a tied election that was decided only after thirty-six ballot tries in the House of Representatives. Jefferson moved into what was called the President's House in the new capital, Federal City, soon to be Washington, D.C. He asked James Madison to be his secretary of state. After Dolley and James moved to Washington in the spring of 1801, they lived in the President's House with Jefferson for almost a year. Dolley could have remained at her own home, as previous government wives had done, but she felt her post was beside James. She also served as the unofficial First Lady for the widowed Jefferson, and managed to maintain order in the official residence.

Federalist newspapers accused Dolley of being Jefferson's mistress. Furious, James planned to duel the accuser. No one could charge his wife with any immorality and get away with it! Jefferson dissuaded him; the stories were false and would die if no attention were paid them.

Dolley's parties and dinners as the secretary's wife were egalitarian. Guests included high-ranking government officials, but tradesmen might also be in attendance. Visitors remarked on how kindly Dolley treated her servants—so much so that it was sometimes difficult to tell who was the mistress and who was the maid.

One of the few things the Madisons disagreed on was her trademark turban, made by winding a length of silk around her head. It quickly became popular as women realized it could salvage a day "when one's hair lay lank or snarled," as Dolley said.

The Madisons bought a house on what would become F Street. They paid $2,375, a high price at the time, and upgraded it by installing indoor plumbing and adding a wine cellar, a coal bin, walnut paneling in the dining room, and a carriage house at the rear. Dolley continued her unconventional ways, doing her own grocery shopping and even dining with James in a newly opened restaurant, the Oyster House. When word came that the famous couple planned to dine there, the manager hastily cleaned up the place and cleared out the prostitutes who hung around.

Dolley made outdoor buffets and barbecues popular. After the Louisiana Territory was purchased from France and became part of the United States in 1803, the Madisons held an outdoor celebration for hundreds of guests.

Dolley wanted to go to New Orleans for the ceremonies annexing the territory to America, but James was too busy to go, and she wouldn't go without him. Never seeing New Orleans was one of her regrets.

When Dolley's sister Anna married, the Madisons had an outdoor reception for which two pits were dug in the backyard: one to roast beef, the other venison. The guests also had roasted corn on the cob, which the Europeans disliked, along with other vegetables and a table of desserts.

Because of Washington's low, swampy location, summers there were difficult. Heat, humidity, and mosquitoes brought James

Madison near to collapse during their first summer in town. From then on, Dolley saw to it that the household moved to Montpelier for the months of August and September. Jefferson began to leave the capital in the summer too, and soon the government began recessing for the season. At Montpelier, Madison did government paperwork and saw official visitors. When any guest kept him up too late, Dolley appeared at the door, bed lamp in hand—a not-so-subtle hint that the visitor should be on his way.

When Jefferson was reelected in 1804, Madison continued as secretary of state, but foreign tensions were building that would erupt into warfare. Britain and France were at war, and both attacked American ships. The British also pressed American sailors into the British navy. Pirates threatened American ships off North Africa, and war with Spain over Florida seemed imminent. In 1807 Jefferson announced an embargo, keeping American ships in port until either England or France agreed to stop the attacks. This angered the New England shipping interests and did little to gain the respect of European nations.

In 1808 James Madison was elected president and inherited a situation that soon resulted in war.

Dolley dressed for the March 4 inauguration in white wool trimmed with purple, and for the ball that evening she wore a low-cut buff-colored velvet gown. She enjoyed being the center of attention, but when her husband felt tired, she left with him at ten o'clock, two hours before the party ended.

Dolley set a new pattern for First Ladies. Both Martha Washington and Abigail Adams had stayed out of the spotlight, and Jefferson's wife had died before his election. Dolley entertained, redecorated official residences, learned to dance and to play cards, and even persuaded her husband to dance in public. At dinners, she always turned the conversation to topics Madison could speak on with authority, impressing guests with his knowledge and ability.

Jefferson, frequently disorganized, didn't vacate the President's House for another week. During his eight years there he had shown little interest in the house itself. Soon after becoming First Lady, Dolley decided to redecorate. She invited key members of Congress to tour the President's House with her so they could see how shabby it was. She said nothing; they appropriated money for repairs and improvement. Indoor plumbing and several rooms were added, the grounds were landscaped, and new china and silverware were purchased.

Dolley then began a series of Wednesday afternoon receptions that became the social events everyone wanted to attend. A band played, refreshments were served, and for a few minutes each week the president himself greeted guests. She began to invite American writers, inventors, and artists, as well as Congressmen and foreign dignitaries. By choosing her guests carefully for small dinners, she was able to win over to Madison's side a group of young Congressmen from the west called the War Hawks.

Attempting to balance the interests of North and South in his cabinet, Madison had chosen weak candidates for secretary of state and secretary of the Navy. James Monroe, again elected governor of Virginia in 1811, was the logical choice for secretary of state, but the two men had been at odds since Monroe briefly supported John Randolph for president in 1808. As war loomed, however, James and Dolley visited the Monroes in Albemarle County, and Monroe agreed to accept the post.

Britain had continued to seize American ships and citizens, despite Madison's warnings. On June 1, 1812, the president asked Congress to declare war on Britain, which it did two weeks later. The country was badly divided; New England refused to cooperate with the federal government, and the army and navy were poorly prepared and ill-equipped. Many feared America would lose the war and be divided among the various European nations.

In addition to the war with England, Dolley had another worry. Her son Payne, now twenty-two, had completed school but had no ambitions. Although he worked occasionally as a clerk, he spent most of his time and money on clothes and women. When Russia offered to mediate negotiations between Britain and America to end the war, Madison made Payne an official member of the delegation to Europe in 1813.

Soon after Payne was sent away, James Madison became seriously ill. For three weeks Dolley would allow no one to see her husband. Then James Monroe was allowed in, and a month later members of Congress. Dolley curtailed all entertaining from then until the end of the war. Her husband's health was far more important.

"Mr. Madison's War," as critics called it, went badly. In 1814 Napoleon was defeated and Britain could throw her full army and navy against America. The British fleet appeared in the Chesapeake Bay, sailing for Baltimore and Washington, and the Madisons were finally forced to abandon the capital city.

After Dolley left with the government papers and presidential portraits, the Madisons were reunited in the Virginia countryside; they later returned to a gutted, burned city. Because the President's House had been burned, the Madison's lived first in Octagon House, then in small rented rooms. The official residence was repaired and painted, becoming the White House.

Peace negotiations were begun, and in 1815 the Treaty of Ghent was signed. Three weeks later, the Battle of New Orleans showed that Americans could decisively defeat British troops. Peace came to America and Europe, and Dolley was invited to Paris, but Madison's ill health kept her in Washington.

Madison recovered after a long stay at Montpelier. The couple enjoyed the last days of his administration, with Dolley continuing her Wednesday receptions. She began packing to leave the

White House at the proper time and in good condition for newly elected President James Monroe and his wife. After Monroe's inauguration, the Madisons retired happily to Montpelier. Dolley helped James sort his business papers and make copies of them.

Only Payne Todd continued to trouble them. Dolley's son had returned from Europe $8,000 in debt, which the Madisons paid. Although he promised to farm Montpelier, he soon left, drifting about the United States, gambling, and running up debts that eventually impoverished his mother.

The Madisons entertained the Marquis de Lafayette on his triumphal visit to America in 1824, and in 1829 Madison was elected as a delegate to write Virginia's new constitution. Dolley, now sixty-one, accompanied James to Richmond for the three-month stay.

James Madison died in 1836 at the age of eighty-five after seven years of relative tranquility at Montpelier. Dolley soon learned she was broke, mainly because of money paid out for her son. Montpelier was sold, and Dolley moved into a rental house in Washington. She continued to have an active social life, though on a somewhat reduced scale, and made trips to New York and Philadelphia. She was invited to the White House by each succeeding president, and entertained at small receptions. Long expelled as a Quaker, Dolley became an Episcopalian in 1842. Impoverished by her son's debts, she accepted an offer from Congress to buy James Madison's presidential papers for $25,000. The money was put in trust for her so that Payne could not get it.

Dolley attended an early demonstration of the telegraph and had a message sent in her name. A seat in the House of Representatives was set aside for her. She attended the inauguration of President Zachary Taylor, who had been born in Orange County, near James Madison's birthplace. She knew well the first twelve U.S. presidents.

Dolley died in July 1849 and was buried in the family plot at Montpelier beside her beloved James Madison.

ANNE NEWPORT ROYALL
1769–1854

Travel Writer

On a June day in 1819, Anne Royall stood before the judge in the Fincastle courthouse in Botetourt County, Virginia, and heard herself legally stripped of all property. Her husband's relatives claimed that his will was invalid and that he had not been of sound mind when he left property to Anne and her niece. Land she had sold was to be taken from the buyers, and money she had spent on herself in the seven years since her husband's death was to be repaid to the estate, in addition to attorneys' fees for the relatives. She was destitute.

Worse, she was sued by the land buyers and her niece's husband. The court ordered seizure of Mrs. Royall's "goods and chattels" and "her body," meaning she was going to debtors prison. Already in her fifties, she simply could not endure what might be the rest of her life in prison. Nor, imprisoned, could she earn money to repay the debt.

Her only recourse was to flee. A stage was leaving the next morning for Alabama, and she managed to get a seat on it. She decided that she would travel and earn her living as a writer. For a woman unknown outside her area, with no important friends, to dream of such a course was fantastic.

Over the next seven years, Anne Royall wrote and published seven travel books, and she met and wrote about every U.S. president from John Adams to Franklin Pierce. She fought government corruption and incompetency, church control of government, and whipping in the Navy. Anne would continue to be on the move for the rest of her life.

Anne Newport was born in Baltimore in 1769, the daughter of William and Mary Newport. When Anne was three and her sister Mary only a baby, the family moved to western Pennsylvania. William Newport, a trader, was often away, leaving his wife and children to tend the farm, look after the animals, and protect themselves from attack. When William was home, he taught Anne to read.

After William's death during the war, Mary married Patrick Butler. The family moved to nearby Hanna's Fort, and Anne soon had a baby brother, James Butler. The end of the war brought independence from Britain, but little changed for frontier settlers. Life was still hard, and they were often attacked by Native Americans. When Anne was thirteen, her stepfather was killed in a vicious attack that destroyed the town she lived in.

Soon afterward, Anne's mother joined a group of refugees moving southward, seeking safety. Anne and James went along, but eleven-year-old Mary stayed behind with friends.

By the time the refugees reached Augusta County, Virginia, Mary Butler was tired of traveling. She accepted a job as cook and housekeeper for the Anderson family, satisfied to have a safe home for herself and her children.

Anne, however, was unhappy in the Virginia community. In Pennsylvania, she had been friends with people of all classes. In Augusta County, she was treated as a servant. This especially rankled her when she had to sit with the servants during the long church services and was ignored afterward as neighbors chatted with each other.

Anne did make one friend, Mrs. William Lewis, who later left Augusta County to join her husband at Sweet Springs, in Botetourt County. Soon Mrs. Butler and eighteen-year-old Anne—less than five feet tall and sometimes mistaken for a child—left the Andersons and walked the 115 miles to Sweet Springs. Here, Mrs. Lewis introduced them to Major William Royall, who hired Mrs. Butler as his housekeeper.

William Royall was descended from one of Virginia's oldest and wealthiest families. He attended law school at William and Mary College, but did not graduate. Shortly before the American Revolution, William's oldest brother died, leaving a daughter, Elizabeth. Female offspring then had no rights of inheritance. When William's father died, William inherited the entire estate. Now wealthy, he bought a sloop, filled it with food, and sent it to the people of Massachusetts, whose ports were closed by the British in 1774. William volunteered as a soldier in the Revolutionary War, serving for seven years without pay, and even furnishing his own horses.

When the war ended, he moved west and bought 846 acres of land on Peters Mountain in Botetourt County where he built a comfortable house. Royall willingly served on juries, helped lay out roads, and made trips back east to persuade the Virginia legislature to fund schools and public improvements on the frontier.

Anne loved her new life on the Royall plantation. William Royall delighted in sharing books with her and discussing them after she'd read them. He also told her about Freemasonry, a group that he felt "lived Christianity rather than preaching it." Anne was convinced, and this belief was to shape her life and her writing. Anne and William rode together about the countryside, and although neighbors soon began predicting a wedding, it was ten years before the two were married in November 1797. She was twenty-eight; he was in his mid-fifties, almost twice her age.

William Royall bought land along the Kanawha River in what later became Charleston, West Virginia. He told Anne that as soon as he could sell the Peters Mountain land, they would move to the new county seat. She longed to go, to see more of the world, but there were no buyers for the Peters Mountain property. Anne managed the farm, turning from crops to sheep, while William retreated more and more into reading and drinking.

In 1806 Anne's niece, Anna Malvina Cowan, came to live with the Royalls. William promised to will her land so she could make a good marriage. Anne would have one-third of his estate and the income for life from the rest. After her death it would go to his great-nephew, William Royall Roane, son of his niece Elizabeth. William had already forgiven a debt of $2,000 to Elizabeth's husband and deeded over to them the James River plantation where they lived, but they were still in debt and desperate to get more from him.

William Roane came for a month's visit and heard gossip that Royall had complained in the tavern of his wife's striking him when he was drunk. Anne was so tiny that she had to have a servant's help to get her drunken husband to bed, so it is unlikely that she hit him. Although Royall displayed no injuries, Roane believed the gossip.

After his visit, Roane wrote a letter criticizing Anne, and William Royall took his great-nephew out of his will. William died in December 1812.

In March 1813, Anne had the will probated, arranged for the sale of the plantation at auction, and left for Charleston with Anna Malvina. Here she began building a tavern and invested in salt mining. The plantation sold at auction for only $500 instead of the expected $5,000, leaving Anne almost penniless. She went into debt for Anna Malvina's wedding, giving her money in lieu of the land that William's will had provided for.

The Roanes contested the will; hearings were scheduled and postponed again and again. Expecting a favorable outcome, Anne secured a loan against the estate to pay off her debts. When the suit was heard in April 1817, neighbors and enemies testified that Royall had been an alcoholic and that Anne had bribed one of the witnesses to the will. Despite this, however, the court ruled that the will was valid.

The Roanes immediately appealed.

While she waited for the next hearing, Anne decided to start seeing the world. She set off for the newly organized Alabama Territory and began writing notes about her journey, which were later gathered into a book, *Letters from Alabama.* As she crossed Tennessee, she recorded that too much whiskey was consumed. She was a teetotaler, having seen alcohol destroy her husband and her own security.

Alabama had been formed of land taken from the Cherokee, who had been expelled to Arkansas and Oklahoma. Exploring one of the abandoned settlements, Anne observed that the Cherokee were like whites, with the same orchards, the same cornfields, and the same houses. Asked whether the Cherokee would be safe from white invasion in Oklahoma, she replied sadly but accurately, "A vain hope!"

Anne met General Andrew Jackson when he passed through Alabama on the way to fight Seminole Indians in Florida. She described him as affable and a kind master to his slaves. Despite his hatred of Native Americans, Jackson had saved the life of a Cherokee baby and adopted him, naming him Lincoyer Jackson.

Anne meticulously recorded the details of life in Alabama: weather, lay of the land, number of inhabitants in each village, and living conditions. She deplored the slavery she saw.

Finally, she had to return to Fincastle for the hearing that dashed all her hopes of money from William's estate. Destitute, she spent the next four years traveling in Alabama, living on the tiny dole from her dower rights. Eventually, even that was cut off.

Anne organized her travel notes into her first book, *Sketches of History, Life, and Manners in the United States,* and she began writing a novel, *The Tennessean.*

Her attorney applied for a pension for Anne as the widow of a Revolutionary War officer. While she waited, she finished her novel and sent it to a Philadelphia publisher. When the pension board wrote in December that they found no record of William Royall's military service, Anne set off for Federal City, as Washington was then called. She would convince the board of her claim and finish her travel book, she decided, planning to sell the book by subscription. Anne stayed several months in Alexandria, Virginia, taking advantage of her husband's Masonic membership for hospitality and help.

Both her books were rejected, and the pension board was still unable to find Royall's records, perhaps because of a fire in Richmond a decade before. Anne set off for Richmond, first by packet boat, the *Mount Vernon,* then by stage. She lacked the five dollars for the coach trip to Richmond until a kind farmer bought her a ticket. In Richmond, she was ostracized by Royall kin but managed to get what she thought were the necessary papers for a pension. She was back in Federal City within a week, penniless. Everywhere she went, she begged for food and continued writing.

Finding shelter from rainfall in a doorway in Alexandria, she met Sally Dorret, who gave Anne a home and became her friend for life.

Again Anne set out to win her pension, but there was another obstacle. The pension only applied if the soldier had married before 1794; Anne's marriage was three years too late. There was still one possibility. When the war was going badly in 1780, Congress promised half pay for life to soldiers who stayed until the end of the war, as William Royall had done, but no money was available at the time. The notes were reduced in value and the date advanced ten years, but they had still not been paid off, though they had been drawing interest. All that was needed was for the present Congress to pass a commutation-of-pay resolution. Anne called on congressmen who told her they would consider voting for the measure. She succeeded also in getting many congressmen to subscribe to the publication of her book.

Meanwhile, she explored Federal City, especially the Capitol, and described with disgust that "grog" was sold not only to workmen finishing the building but also to congressmen themselves.

The commutation-of-pay bill was rejected. Another hope dashed. Anne remained in Washington during the summer and early fall of election year 1824 and met three of the four candidates for president: John Calhoun, Henry Clay, and John Quincy Adams. All three subscribed to her book; Adams gave her money in advance. He also introduced her to his father, former President John Adams, who was sick at home in Massachusetts, and sent Anne to meet his wife, who befriended the author.

In October, Anne watched as the Marquis de Lafayette made his triumphal visit to Washington. Afterward, she talked her way past his guard and told the French soldier that her husband had served with him during the American Revolution. Lafayette offered her money, but she asked instead for a letter describing her husband's service. Lafayette gladly obliged. He and Royall had shared a belief in Freemasonry as well as the fight for independence. She used the letter as an introduction to important people. She hoped it would convince Congress to grant her a pension, but it did not.

Anne moved on to Baltimore shortly thereafter. Baltimore was a disappointment to Anne, except that she noted hearing a "new song, '*The Star-Spangled Banner*,' written at Fort McHenry." She managed to get a free ride to Philadelphia, then America's largest city, which also disappointed her. Earning only one subscription for her book, she walked the streets begging until her feet bled.

Anne pilloried in print those who were rude to her. When asked why she didn't wait until someone was dead to criticize, she answered, "I might die first."

New York made up for any slights. Here she met editors, newspapermen, and Masons sympathetic to her cause. A theatrical benefit was given for her, and despite a blizzard, Masons and their families showed up. At the end of the evening, she was given $180 to pay for her travel to New England.

On the way she saw the almost completed Erie Canal, toured the U.S. Arsenal in Springfield, Massachusetts, and visited the school for deaf mutes founded by Thomas Gallaudet in Hartford, Connecticut.

In Boston, Anne spent hours with former President Adams, then eighty-nine years old. She also met his cousin, Hannah Adams. Author of *History of the Jews* and *A Dictionary of Religion,* Hannah was the first American woman to make writing her profession.

Anne returned to New York from Boston to find that her printer was dying and her book had not gone to press. Hearing of a possible printer in New Haven, she hastened there, and after some months was able to get *Sketches* printed on credit. Yale College paid for binding the book. Anne took as many copies as she could carry and set off to sell them, arranging for others to be shipped to her in New York.

Despite a good review by Mordecai Noah of the *National Advocate,* the book sold poorly in New York. Anne returned to Boston, where the book sold so briskly the printers could scarcely keep up with demand.

Anne now began to have good reviews and good sales everywhere, especially in New England, but she got involved in the nationwide struggle between the Masons and Protestants. Many prominent Americans were Masons, including George Washington. In 1826 William Morgan claimed to be writing a book exposing the secrets of Masonry. It turned out to be a reprint of an earlier book, but Masons in New York were furious. Morgan, a thief, was jailed, but he was taken from the jail at night and disappeared. Three Masons were convicted for abducting him. Anti-Mason sentiment flared first in New York and later across America, fueled by evangelical preachers. Anne, whose husband had been a Mason, attended church every Sunday, regardless of denomination, but spoke out against aggressive evangelists. For this, she paid dearly.

In Burlington, Vermont, Anne entered Mr. Hickock's general store to sell him a book. Instead, he shoved her down a ten-foot flight of stairs into the snow, breaking her leg in two places. Anne's attorney, the former governor of Vermont, sued Hickock, who first claimed a dog had pushed her down the steps, but later settled. Anne, an invalid for five painful weeks, finally slipped out of Burlington. She went first to New York, then took a stage to Philadelphia, eventually reaching Washington, where her friend Sally Dorret, now Mrs. Stack, took care of her.

Still in pain, Anne was carried to the Senate and the House of Representatives to hear debates. She noted that grog was still being sold. At the State Department, she complained that valuable books were lying dusty on the floor. Word spread that Anne Royall was rampaging through Washington, and uneasy clerks fled from her.

Anne published *The Black Book I* and *II*. Both full of gossipy descriptions of famous Americans, they became best-sellers. Anne was finally solvent, but she began receiving anonymous hate mail. In Pennsylvania, she tacked the worst of these letters outside the newspaper office for all to read.

Back again in Washington, she wrote *Black Book III* in six weeks and began work on *Mrs. Royall's Pennsylvania*. For Andrew Jackson's Inaugural in 1829, Anne indulged herself by spending two dollars for a dress. She described the event in detail, including the mass of people, and concluded that if she were ever caught in such a crowd again, it would be by accident.

Her reputation as a Masonic supporter spread, and one Sunday morning she was awakened by children throwing rocks at her window. Two of her windows were smashed. When she protested to the parents, they did nothing, but that night and for many nights thereafter, they met beneath her window, praying aloud and harassing her whenever she ventured outside. She swore at her tormentors and was arrested as a "common scold." The group attempted to charge her with drunkenness, but failed. No witnesses could be found who had ever seen her drinking alcohol.

Despite having high-ranking Jackson associates as attorneys and character witnesses, and despite her own plea for freedom of speech, Anne was found guilty and fined ten dollars, an amount quickly paid by two newspaper reporters. She was the only American ever tried on such a charge. The well-attended trial was a sensation, and the publicity helped sell many of her books.

Anne Royall was now known throughout America. When she announced plans for a Southern tour and travel book, she was given free rides on mail coaches. Her reception, however, was controversial. In Charlottesville, Virginia, students rushed her coach, then forced the door of the inn she was staying at and shoved obscene notes under her door. Two days later in Farmville, she was greeted by John Randolph, who had bought land once owned by Royall heirs.

Anne liked North Carolina, but some of its inhabitants didn't like her description of them as snuff-users. In Charleston, South Carolina, she was snubbed by the editor of the *Mercury*, but welcomed by the Jewish family who owned the *Southern Patriot*. She found Georgia hot but interesting. Although bookshops in Mobile sold her books, she considered the town itself unsafe, full of pirates and ruffians. She left the city quickly, taking the *Mount Vernon* to

New Orleans, the very boat she'd taken on her first trip from Washington to Richmond.

After visiting New Orleans, which she found delightful but expensive, Anne traveled upriver to St. Louis. She left quickly because of harassment by religious zealots, crossing over to Indiana to visit her half brother, James Butler. Anne saw her mother for the last time in Illinois, then traveled to Pittsburgh, where she was beaten on the head with a cowhide by Charles Plumb, an anti-Mason. He was fined twenty dollars. She escaped serious injury, she said, because of the heavy padding in her bonnet.

Anne returned to Washington, published the three-volume *Southern Tour*, and, at age sixty-one, began yet another career: newspaper publishing. On December 3, 1831, the first issue of *Paul Pry,* her gossipy four-page paper, appeared. Anne and Sally Stack begged for donations to keep the paper going and did most of the work themselves: writing, stacking, and selling.

Anne took on a new enemy, the Bank of the United States, which she and President Jackson believed was responsible for the ruin of many Americans. She was surprised that other newspapers didn't attack the bank until she discovered that many of them had gotten big loans from the institution. She saw this as bribery. She also exposed nepotism in government and demanded a sewer system for Washington to prevent the cholera that regularly struck the city.

Lack of money continued to be a problem for Anne. When *Paul Pry* went broke, Anne and Sally Stack took a break from publication, then, with new donations, began another newspaper, *The Huntress.* Anne decried the flogging of sailors, and after a congressional investigation, the practice was ended.

Former President John Quincy Adams, then a congressman, regularly introduced a pension bill for Revolutionary War widows; in February 1848, he collapsed and died just after introducing it for the last time. That July, however, Congress passed the bill, and Anne was granted $480 per year for life.

After receiving the pension for only six years, Anne died on October 1, 1854, at age eighty-five. She was buried in an unmarked grave in the Congressional Cemetery. The *Washington Sentinel* wrote of her three days later: "She was a woman of considerable literary attainments and benevolence, and of strict integrity."

PRISCILLA COOPER TYLER

1816–1889

From Actress to Acting First Lady

On a March evening in 1837, Priscilla Cooper appeared on a Richmond stage as Desdemona, a performance that was to change the direction of her life. Her father, the renowned Shakespearean actor Thomas Cooper, played Othello. The two had already acted opposite each other in a variety of dramas, appearing on stages from Albany, New York, to Charleston, South Carolina. Priscilla had performed onstage in Norfolk and Petersburg as well.

That night a young man in the Richmond audience saw Priscilla and fell in love. When she came onstage, the audience gave polite applause before she had spoken a line, as was the custom. Young Robert Tyler continued standing and applauding long after others had sat down. Priscilla could not help noticing her admirer but went on with the performance.

Afterward, Tyler went backstage, introduced himself, and asked Priscilla's father's for permission to court her. She must marry him, he insisted. Despite their different backgrounds, Priscilla fell in love with Robert Tyler and agreed to become his wife. In marrying him, she would be leaving the stage and joining one of Virginia's most famous families.

Priscilla Cooper was born in New York in 1816, the third child of an unlikely pair. Her mother, Mary Fairlie, was a member of a wealthy and politically prominent New York family. Mary had had many suitors, including the writer Washington Irving. Thomas Cooper, a thirty-six-year-old actor, was a widower who had immigrated from England at age twenty. He was dashing, handsome, and something of a celebrity, but the Fairlies considered acting an uncertain, unsuitable profession for their daughter to depend on. Despite family objections, Mary and Thomas were married in 1812. The couple eventually had seven children.

Besides being an actor, Thomas Cooper was a high-stakes gambler, which affected the family fortunes more than his choice of profession did. He once lost $1,200, the entire evening's income from his theater performance, on a hand of cards; on another occasion, he won a cottage and garden on the Delaware River in Bristol, Pennsylvania. His wife Mary liked the place, so the family moved there, away from New York City, in 1819.

The wealthy and famous soon found their way to the Coopers' home, including Washington Irving, Martin van Buren, and Joseph Bonaparte, brother of Napoleon and former king of Naples and Spain.

Thomas Cooper had been adopted as a child by William Godwin, who had unconventional ideas, especially about rearing children. Cooper used the same ideas in educating his seven children. He built a second house on the property for the children and their governess to live in, joined to the original cottage by a walkway. He and his wife lived in the cottage and sometimes invited the children over to dine or to have dessert. Both Coopers supplemented the governess's instruction, reading poetry and other literature to their children, teaching them to write, to speak French, and to carry on adult conversations.

Early on, Priscilla began keeping a journal and writing lively letters, but she rebelled at learning mathematics and was seldom disciplined for getting into childhood trouble.

Parents who oppose a marriage are often reconciled with the offenders when grandchildren arrive; Grandmother Fairlie, Mary's mother, was no exception. She visited the Coopers and invited the children to visit her in the city. Priscilla and Mary Grace thought their grandmother haughty and stern, but they enjoyed their trips to the city, especially going to the theater. Priscilla began to write plays and produce them using family and neighbors as players. She said later that when she needed to portray an empress or queen onstage, she thought back to her grandmother and copied the older woman's gestures and manner.

In a letter to Washington Irving, Mary Cooper described her children. Of Priscilla she wrote: "She is all talent—that is, in regard to sprightliness of mind, cleverness in writing, and fun and drollery in everything; but so incapable of application that she has not of what is technically called accomplishments a single one. . . . She is not beautiful, but there is something very piquant in her countenance."

Priscilla was in her teens when her grandfather died, followed soon afterward by the deaths of her two infant brothers. Mary Cooper became despondent and fell ill. Her husband provided little help or comfort because he was frequently away performing. But he was past his peak of popularity, and younger actors had caught America's attention. Although Thomas's acting tours no longer brought in the income the family needed, he was not ready to quit the stage.

In 1833, Mary Cooper died at age forty-three. Her mother, the widowed Mrs. Fairlie, offered to come and live with the family or to take the children with her to New York. Thomas Cooper rejected both offers and tried to keep the household going with the help of a servant and the older girls, but times were hard, and he fell deeper into debt.

Theater friends in New York arranged two benefits for Cooper, in remembrance of his years in the theater. They raised $7,000, which he considered a pittance. Cooper accepted the money, but instead of retiring gracefully as his friends expected, he arranged a theatrical tour. Priscilla went along, playing the various female parts opposite her father, so that the receipts would not have to be shared with another actress.

Acting then was considered a scandalous occupation for a young lady, but Priscilla's innocence and grace overcame critics. Perhaps many realized that she was onstage at first only to financially support her father. Gradually, she began to enjoy the attention and celebrity, but she longed for the security of a home and family. While in Richmond, Priscilla visited a friend who had married a member of one of Virginia's wealthiest families, the Randolphs, and lived at Wilton, a fine estate. Priscilla envied her and wrote her sister that if someone with a large estate in Virginia and a good name should fall in love with her, she would not refuse a proposal.

Soon afterward, she met Robert Tyler, but despite her wish for security, she had mixed feelings about marrying him. According to his letters, she refused him six times. Finally, while visiting a friend in Petersburg, Virginia, in March 1839, she agreed to marry him. The wedding took place several months later.

The Tyler family, which had owned property in Virginia since the 1600s, had been prominent politically for several generations. Robert's father, John Tyler, had been governor of Virginia several times as well as a U.S. senator. Robert, who was studying law at William and Mary College, had a bright career ahead of him.

The Tylers made no objection to their son marrying a poor actress. John Tyler made the trip to Bristol, New York, to be his son's best man at the wedding. Robert's mother, Letitia Tyler, had suffered a stroke and didn't travel.

The newlyweds spent a monthlong honeymoon with Robert's sister Mary and her husband at their Charles City, Virginia, plantation, then moved to Williamsburg, where they shared a house with Robert's parents. Robert and his father had law offices in the house as well. Priscilla, using her playwriting and drama skills, helped Robert write his speeches when he appeared in court.

Priscilla was expecting her first child in 1840, and Robert was planning to open a law office in Petersburg, when their life changed abruptly. John Tyler was nominated as William Henry Harrison's vice president on the Whig ticket, running with the slogan, "Tippecanoe and Tyler Too." Priscilla wrote everyone she knew, urging them to vote for her father-in-law. When the Whigs won, Robert abandoned the idea of moving to Petersburg. He would help his father, who declined to move to Washington and continued to live quietly in Williamsburg.

In April 1841 President Harrison died after only a month in office. John Tyler was now president, and because his wife was an invalid, Priscilla, at twenty-two, became the official White House hostess.

President Tyler disagreed with his party on many issues and became the center of controversy in Washington. Mobs burned him in effigy after he vetoed a tariff bill, but he was unfailingly courteous to friend and enemy alike, and Priscilla wanted to please him. She called him "Father" and said later that she loved him as much as she did her own father. But she felt overwhelmed by the dinners, calls, receptions, and other duties she faced in the White House, so she turned for help to another Virginian and accomplished hostess, former First Lady Dolley Madison. Mrs. Madison was pleased to offer suggestions and support.

At cabinet dinners, protocol required that Secretary of State

Daniel Webster escort Priscilla. During the first of these dinners she attended, she fainted from nervousness, and Webster gathered her up in his arms to take her away from the table. Impetuously, her husband Robert dashed a pitcher of cold water on her to awaken her, splashing both Priscilla and Webster. After this inauspicious start, she and Webster became good friends, and she was soon writing her sister about chatting with important men and sitting across the table from the president.

Priscilla's early experience meeting celebrities in her family home helped her in the White House. Nobility, military heroes, politicians, and ordinary people came to receptions and dinners. Charles Dickens and Washington Irving dined at the White House on the same evening, and she wrote her sister that both were talking with her at the same time. She was delighted to see Irving, an old friend, who had just been appointed minister to Spain. Dickens, she thought, was a bit frumpy and not as interesting in person as his books were. Newspapers described the event the following day, commenting on Priscilla's graciousness and charm.

In June 1842 Priscilla and Robert became the parents of a daughter, named Letitia for her grandmother, President Tyler's wife, who died a few months later.

The following year, President Tyler quietly married Julia Gardiner, a wealthy young woman thirty years his junior, who became a lively First Lady. Priscilla and Robert moved to Philadelphia where he planned to establish a law practice. They returned to the White House for a gala ball that Julia arranged as a farewell party for her husband at the end of his term. He had bought a large Virginia plantation he called Sherwood Forest and retired there with Julia and his second family.

Priscilla had difficulty adjusting to life in the cramped quarters in Philadelphia. Her husband spent his time studying, and she had two small children and a third on the way. This was quite a comedown from the comfort of Williamsburg and the excitement of Washington.

Her third child was a son, named John Tyler IV. Six months later the Tylers' first daughter became ill. They took her to Virginia hoping she would recover, but she died and was buried in the Tyler cemetery in New Kent County. Little more than a year later, little John died suddenly. Robert sent Priscilla and Letitia to Alabama to visit her sister and recover from this double grief.

The Tylers had another daughter, Grace, in 1846, and a son, Thomas, in 1847. Two years later, Priscilla grieved again when little Thomas and the grandfather he was named for died within a month of each other.

The next decade was a time of prosperity and happiness for Priscilla and Robert. Two more daughters and a son, Robert Tyler Jr., were born to them. In 1856 Robert campaigned for James Buchanan, who was running for the presidency. After Buchanan's election, Robert was offered an appointment as Minister to Switzerland but, to Priscilla's disappointment, he declined. He was chosen chairman of the Pennsylvania Democratic Committee and his name was suggested as vice-presidential candidate in 1860; he declined that as well. As a split between North and South became obvious, Robert sided with Virginia and the South. When he spoke out for states' rights, vigilantes planned to lynch him, and he fled to Virginia.

Priscilla packed a few belongings, left the rest to be sold for Robert's debts, and followed him to Virginia before a blockade stopped travel between North and South. The Tyler family was split along with the nation. Most of the children accompanied Priscilla, but her daughter Elizabeth remained behind with Priscilla's sister Julia, and the family dog was left at the boat landing with neighborhood children.

Priscilla arrived in Richmond in May 1861 with her children and trunks, but Robert was not at the train station. She hired a carriage and drove to the Exchange Hotel where the family had stayed on other occasions. Robert had just arrived at the hotel from Sherwood Forest, the Tyler country estate. He had not received Priscilla's letter telling of her travel plans. Thinking Richmond, the Confederate capital, was in danger of invasion by the Union, Robert made plans for the family to go to Sherwood Forest for safety.

The Union invasion was turned back by the Battle of Bull Run, a victory for the Confederacy. Priscilla and the children joined Robert in Richmond, where he worked as register of the treasury under the direction of Confederate President Jefferson Davis.

Robert's father, the former President Tyler, was elected to the Confederate Provisional Congress. He was in Richmond early in 1862 to participate in a congressional meeting when he collapsed and died suddenly. His widow, Julia Gardiner Tyler, was left with seven children, the youngest only two. Although she longed to return to her mother in New York, she decided to stay on at Sherwood Forest, which Union forces protected.

In the spring of 1862, when a fever struck the family at Sherwood Forest, Priscilla went to the plantation to care for them. After the epidemic subsided, she returned to Richmond, which was once more threatened with invasion. This time the Union army was beaten back to within sight of the city.

At Robert's suggestion, Priscilla took the children to be with her sister in Alabama, thinking it safer than Virginia. Robert accompanied them as far as Marietta, Georgia, then turned back to continue working with President Davis. The Tyler's' second daughter married in Alabama in November 1863. The other three daughters remained there when Priscilla returned to Richmond with baby Robert, whom they called Robbie.

By late 1864 Richmond was again besieged, and again Robert sent Priscilla to Alabama for safety. But Union forces moved on

Alabama in April 1865, and Priscilla faced the challenge of many other Southerners: how to protect her home from marauding soldiers. Priscilla's and her sister Mary's children were sent to Georgia, and the men went to defend Montgomery, the Alabama capital. Priscilla and Mary were each left to defend a plantation. Mary was briefly held at gunpoint by Union soldiers, and all around them fires lighted the night as houses and crops were burned.

Determined to get military protection for her son-in-law's plantation, Priscilla started walking toward the army. By sheer good luck, the first officer she met was from Philadelphia and had known Robert Tyler when the family had lived there. He gave her a protection order, which she had to show repeatedly over the next few days. The house was spared, but the plantation was devastated. The troops burned more than 2,500 bushels of corn and all the rice and dried beans in storage houses. They raided the smokehouse and stole all the meat. The family faced starvation.

The end of the war came quickly in Virginia at about the same time. President Davis dismissed all his staff, including Robert Tyler, who went to Danville and surrendered to Union authorities.

When word spread of Robert's precarious financial condition, former President Buchanan sent a check for $1,000, but Robert returned it. He had lost everything but his honor, he wrote; he could not let himself be supported by others. In a later letter, he expressed gratitude that none of his family had been killed during the war, and that they were setting to work to support themselves. He described Priscilla as an excellent mother who had shaped the children's character.

The Tylers were penniless. Robert joined Priscilla in Alabama, but quickly realized he couldn't earn a living as a lawyer there. For seven years he was editor of the *Montgomery Register* and chairman of the State Democratic Committee, trying to ease the worst of Reconstruction. The Tylers, who had lived in the White House, made do in rented rooms. Their daughter Letitia became a teacher and remained single; the other daughters married well.

Then death closed in on Priscilla once more. Within a few years her sister Julia and Julia's only son died, as did another sister and a brother-in-law. Then, in December 1877, her beloved Robert died suddenly, much as his father had. He was in court when he began to feel dizzy and was taken home. He died that evening, of what was probably a stroke.

Without Robert, Priscilla was not only grief-stricken but destitute. Priscilla's brother-in-law Allan Campbell, grieving the loss of his wife Julia and his son, came to the rescue. The wealthy man hired her son Robbie as his private secretary and supported Priscilla financially. She spent winters in Alabama with her widowed sister Mary Grace and summers in New York with Allan Campbell. The two formed a devoted friendship, exchanging letters when they were separated and spending days at the beach with family during the summer. Campbell enjoyed sharing his wealth, and for the first time in her life, Priscilla was without money worries.

In 1889, Priscilla became ill while in New York. She died peacefully in the early morning of December 29, at the age of seventy-three. Newspaper articles telling of her death described her beauty, her charm, and her acting ability, and recounted her eventful life.

BELLE BOYD AND ELIZABETH VAN LEW

1844–1900 AND 1818–1900

Virginia's Lady Spies

*T*wo Virginia women were famous spies during the Civil War. Belle Boyd, more flamboyant and better known, spied against Union troops for Stonewall Jackson. Her side lost the war, but Belle Boyd herself went on to lead a long and interesting life. Elizabeth Van Lew, on the other hand, aided the Union prisoners held by Confederates in Richmond and later helped the Union invaders who conquered Virginia's capital city. She was on the winning side, but after the war she chose to live on in Richmond, despised by her neighbors and almost forgotten by the victors she had assisted.

Isabel "Belle" Boyd was born May 9, 1844, in Martinsburg, Virginia (now West Virginia), to well-to-do parents. Her father ran a general store and managed a tobacco plantation. At age twelve Belle was sent to Mount Washington Female College in Baltimore; at sixteen, according to the custom of the day, she made her entry into society in Washington, D.C.

Then war came. Belle's father volunteered as a private in the Second Virginia Infantry. Martinsburg, on the border between the North and the South, changed hands several times.

Belle Boyd

Elizabeth Van Lew

When Union troops took over the town and searched and pillaged the Boyd home, Belle shot a soldier, who died a few hours later. The Boyd house was surrounded and Belle's every move was observed, but her faithful servant Eliza Hopewell carried reports of Union troop numbers from Belle to General J. E. B. Stuart. The Union authorities thought incorrectly that slaves would turn against their Southern owners and therefore never suspected or stopped them. Belle, however, made the mistake of not encoding her messages. One note was picked up and she was warned to cease spying or face death.

Belle went to live with a relative in Front Royal, Virginia, to help tend the wounded. She also became a courier. Attempting a visit to her mother in Martinsburg, she was taken off the train and escorted to the quarters of General John A. Dix in Baltimore. Because Belle had a Federal pass to go through the lines, General Dix released her and sent her home. Again she was kept under surveillance and forbidden to go beyond the town limits.

Belle and her mother decided to return to Front Royal, but when they reached Winchester, they found that travel any farther was prohibited. They stayed in a cottage on the grounds of a hotel where Federal troops were quartered. Belle eavesdropped on their meeting, then rode to tell General Turner Ashby of the planned troop movements. This time she was not caught.

Belle was later asked to carry letters to the Confederate army. She put one letter in a basket she was to carry, with a note unintentionally incriminating a Union lieutenant, and gave another to Eliza. Someone alerted Federal officers, and Belle, Eliza, and the lieutenant were stopped. Again, Belle was let off with a warning, but the lieutenant was punished for carrying a parcel for Belle and for having Southern newspapers in his possession.

Her most daring feat occurred on May 23, 1862. Belle was in Front Royal when she was given a note for Stonewall Jackson.

She slipped outside, got past the picket guards, and ran for Southern lines. Unfortunately, she was wearing a white apron over her dress, which made her more visible to troops on both sides. Belle was shot at, fell, got up, and made it to Jackson. She told him that the Union forces were so small that he could easily defeat them in battle. Jackson was able to win the following day and retreat back across the mountains to safety.

Belle was taken prisoner, betrayed by a woman she had befriended, but again she was released. The Northern press started calling her the "Sesesh Cleopatra." "Sesesh" was slang for a person who supported secession of the Southern states.

She was finally caught after asking a friendly man in a Confederate uniform to take a note to Jackson for her. The "Confederate" went straight to Union General Franz Siegel, who sent the letter to Secretary of War Edwin Stanton.

This time Belle was arrested and imprisoned for a month in Old Capitol, a prison in Washington, D.C. She contracted typhoid due to poor sanitation in the prison. Despite this, Belle sang cheerfully, and crowds gathered outside her prison cell. Although no charges were filed against her, authorities decided to send her to Fitchburg prison. Her father came to Washington and arranged for her to be transferred instead to Fort Monroe at Hampton, Virginia. He became ill while in Washington, and Belle begged for permission to visit him, but was refused. She never saw him again.

Fort Monroe was under the command of Benjamin Butler, called "The Beast" because of his treatment of Southerners. Among other offenses, he had had a man in New Orleans hanged for cutting down an American flag. Belle made the mistake of speaking sharply to General Butler, who then ordered her banishment aboard a ship. Her trunk was searched by an officer who found a uniform and General Jackson's field glasses. Belle surrendered letters she was carrying and $3,000 in Confederate money.

The captain who was searching her scornfully returned the nearly worthless money. Belle did not reveal that she was also carrying $5,000 in United States money.

As Belle's boat was heading for Richmond, General Butler changed his mind and sent another boat after her, with orders to return her to prison. Again Belle charmed her captors and the captain ignored the signal from the second boat.

Belle fled to Georgia and Alabama and was then assigned as a messenger on a boat running the blockade. She was too sick to take the first boat and almost missed the second at Wilmington, North Carolina. Finally she got on the *Greyhound*, which put to sea the night before Belle's twentieth birthday. The *Greyhound* was pursued and shot at by the *Connecticut*. Expecting capture, the crew pushed bales of cotton overboard rather than have them captured by the Federals, and Belle burned the letters she was carrying. Shortly, however, crew from the *Connecticut* boarded the *Greyhound*.

A young ensign from the *Connecticut*, Samuel Hardinge, fell in love with Belle. When the ship docked in Boston, the captain of the *Greyhound* escaped and Hardinge arranged for Belle to escape to Canada. For this, he was dismissed from the navy and imprisoned.

From Canada, Belle took passage to England. Hardinge later joined her, and they were married in 1864. On a trip back to America, Hardinge was imprisoned and then released. He returned to England, but died soon after the birth of their daughter, Grace.

Belle was alone and destitute in a foreign country. To support herself, she wrote an account of her wartime experiences, *Belle Boyd in Camp and Prison*, which was published in England in 1865.

The following year, Belle returned to the United States and toured as an actress, using the name Nina Benjamin. In 1869 John Hammond saw her on the stage in New Orleans, fell in love with her, and within two months had married her. Hammond, an Englishman, had been an officer during the Crimean War and had fought for the U.S. Army in 1861. After the Civil War he remained in America as a coffee and tea salesman.

Over the next fifteen years, the Hammonds had four children, one of whom died in infancy. Then, in 1884, Belle fell in love with Nat High, an actor only four years older than her daughter Grace and sued Hammond for divorce. She was granted custody of the children, and received the Hammonds' Dallas house. Hammond set up trust funds for the children, including Grace, Belle's daughter from her first marriage.

The following year Belle married High, but he was unable to support the family, so Belle began giving dramatic recitations about being a spy. After every show, veterans would come up to talk to her, and she gave a portion of her receipts to veterans groups in both the North and the South. She was so popular that fake "Belles" began to appear, and she had to carry credentials to prove her identity.

Belle was appearing in Kilbourne, Wisconsin, on June 9, 1900, when she had a heart attack. She died that night, at the age of fifty-six. Four days later, the most famous Southern spy was buried in Kilbourne, in Union territory.

Virginia's other famous woman spy, Elizabeth Van Lew, was born on October 15, 1818, in Richmond, the first of three children of John and Eliza Baker Van Lew. John Van Lew was from New York, and his wife from Philadelphia.

The owner of five hardware stores, John Van Lew prospered in Richmond. He bought Church Hill, a three-story mansion on East Grace Street, and it was in that home that Elizabeth was to spend her life.

The Van Lews made friends among prominent Richmond families, including the Marshalls, Lees, and Wickhams, and participated in popular social outings, such as the annual summer trip to

White Sulfur Springs in what is now West Virginia. Elizabeth, or Lizzie as she was called, was sent to Philadelphia for school.

John Van Lew died in 1843, when Lizzie was twenty-five. He left his real estate to his wife, and a $10,000 endowment to each of his three children, a sizable fortune then. Eliza built two houses across the street from Church Hill, which she rented for income. Lizzie, who had become a passionate abolitionist, persuaded her mother to free their nine slaves and hire them back as servants.

After the execution of John Brown in 1859, Lizzie became even more opposed to slavery, and when war came in 1861, she was determined to do everything in her power to see the Confederacy defeated. Although she and her family had been popular, when her attitude became known, her neighbors considered her a traitor and excluded her from all social events.

The Van Lews owned a small farm on the James River, which Lizzie began using as a transfer point for information. She would use baskets of eggs to send messages to the Federal forces at Fort Monroe in Hampton. One egg in each group contained her messages, torn into small pieces and inserted into the shell.

In July 1861, more than 600 Union prisoners captured at the Battle of Bull Run were brought to Richmond. Lizzie immediately visited Harwood Warehouse, where the prisoners were kept, offering food and books to the soldiers.

In January 1862, Paul Joseph Revere, grandson of famous midnight rider Paul Revere, was one of a group of prisoners moved from Harwood to the jail in Henrico. Miss Van Lew visited the jail, again bringing food and books. Revere's group was exchanged for a group of Confederate prisoners, and Revere wrote to his family, telling them of Lizzie's aid.

Another warehouse became Libby Prison, housing thousands of Union officers and soldiers. Lizzie began visiting the prison, dressed shabbily, singing nonsensically, and pretending to be dim-witted.

People began to refer to her as "Crazy Bet," but some officers weren't fooled and watched her movements closely.

After the Seven Days' Battle in the summer of 1862, wounded men from both armies poured into Richmond. While most women of the city tended the Confederates, Elizabeth and her mother cared for the Federal soldiers.

The Van Lews had sent one of their servants, Mary Van Lew Bowser, to be educated at a Quaker school in Philadelphia. In 1863 Elizabeth arranged through a friend for Mary to work for Jefferson Davis and his wife, Varina, cautioning Mary to pretend to be illiterate and to listen carefully to everything she overheard. Mary became an alert, valuable spy.

Early in 1864, 103 prisoners managed to dig a tunnel and escape from Libby Prison. They headed for the Union army in Williamsburg and to many safe houses in the Richmond area. The Van Lew mansion was one of these, but it was unusable that night because Elizabeth's brother, who had been drafted into the Confederate Army, had deserted and was hiding out. Lizzie was with him at one of the other safe houses, and the servants would not allow anyone into the Van Lew mansion without her.

Elizabeth began a correspondence with General Benjamin Butler, urging a raid on Richmond to free the many Union prisoners. Butler sent her letter to the secretary of war, who arranged for a force of 3,500 cavalrymen to march on the city, led by General Judson Kilpatrick and Colonel Ulric Dahlgren. The group split, with Kilpatrick heading south, Dahlgren southwest. When Dahlgren reached the James River, it was impassable. Angry, he attacked farms and the canal and hanged his scout. Meanwhile, Kilpatrick's attack was stopped by the home guard, and the alarm was sounded. He retreated southeastward. When Dahlgren's troops followed, Dahlgren rode out in front, confronted the Confederates near the Mattaponi River, and was shot. One hundred thirty-five of his soldiers and forty free blacks were captured. Dahlgren's artificial leg was taken as a souvenir, and he was buried in a shallow grave.

Confederate President Jefferson Davis had Dahlgren's body brought to Richmond and secretly buried in Oakwood Cemetery. A Unionist who witnessed the burial reported to Elizabeth Van Lew, who arranged for another burial. The exhumed corpse was placed in a wagon, driven past Confederates to a farm north of Richmond, and reburied.

When the Dahlgren family requested the body from President Davis, the grave was found to be empty. After the war Elizabeth Van Lew told the family where the body could be found.

On April 2, 1865, President Davis and his cabinet fled from Richmond to Danville just ahead of Federal troops. As they retreated, the Confederates burned supplies in warehouses. When the wind changed, the fire spread to the city, burning the business district and many houses. Residents fled and looters ran rampant.

The next day Union troops entered the city, and a contingent was sent to protect Elizabeth Van Lew's house. She was not at home, however, but was picking through the ruins of the former Confederate War Department.

Within a week, Lee had surrendered at Appomattox, and the war was finally over. Like most other Southerners, the Van Lews were destitute. Moreover, they were friendless, especially after it was revealed that Elizabeth had paid workers at the arsenal to sabotage munitions to be used by Confederate soldiers. She had betrayed her city, her fellow Virginians, and all of the South, and had put the army in danger of being killed by their own weapons. When her mother died, Elizabeth said that they lacked enough friends to be pallbearers.

But she had friends in the North. Soon after Ulysses Grant became president in 1869, he named Elizabeth Van Lew postmistress for Richmond at a salary of $1,200 per year as payment for her help. She held the office for eight years and apparently ran the post office efficiently. Even her enemies said as much.

The next administration, however, did not reappoint her postmistress. Instead, she was made a clerk and moved to the Washington post office. She was very unhappy there and didn't get along well with other employees. After two years Elizabeth returned to Richmond, jobless and destitute. A constant complainer, she alienated even her niece who came to help her, and complained about church members, neighbors, and even the United States government, which she felt had not adequately rewarded her for her wartime service.

Elizabeth spent her time writing letters begging for money. One of these was sent to the Revere family, who joined with other Northerners to raise funds to support her and, after her death, to place a stone at her grave. Elizabeth Van Lew died on September 25, 1900, a little over two months after the death of Belle Boyd.

The Van Lew mansion, where Lizzie had hidden Union prisoners and runaways, stood vacant until it was torn down in 1911 to make space for an elementary school.

MAGGIE LENA WALKER
1867–1934

Banker and Philanthropist

Sixteen-year-old Maggie Mitchell and nine of her class-mates at Armstrong Normal School were determined that their 1883 high school graduation ceremony would take place in the Richmond Theater where white students graduated, not at a church where Richmond officials insisted it must be held.

When the black students presented their case to the white faculty of the school, the principal and superintendent told the young delegation that they should consider themselves lucky to be graduating at all. Their ancestors had never had such an opportunity.

Times had changed and slavery had ended, the group argued. Of course they had opportunities their ancestors didn't have. Now their parents paid taxes the same as white parents, so they should have the same schooling and graduation ceremony as the white students.

The Richmond Theater management agreed to hold the graduation ceremony in the building but said the black students and their families would have to sit in the balcony, not on the main floor of the theater.

Maggie Lena Walker

The students persisted. There wasn't enough room in the balcony, and it was a matter of fairness, they said. When the theater management refused to budge on the seating arrangement, Maggie Mitchell and her classmates boycotted the public graduation, and their ceremony was held finally at the school itself. They had not gotten what they'd sought, but they did gain public recognition and made their point: Segregation of the races was unfair.

Maggie was born on July 15, 1867, only two years after the end of the Civil War, which had destroyed much of Richmond. Her mother, Elizabeth Draper, had been a slave owned by the Van Lew family. The Van Lews had freed Elizabeth before the Civil War, but she continued working for them as a house servant. Maggie's father, Eccles Cuthbert, was a white newspaperman from New York who made frequent trips to Richmond. He never married Elizabeth Draper, for interracial marriages were then illegal in Virginia.

Before Maggie was a year old, Elizabeth married William Mitchell, the butler in the Van Lew house. Maggie Lena Draper took Mitchell's name. Many people thought he was Maggie's father, and as a child, she thought so too. She was allowed to wander about the Van Lew mansion, and learned to read early.

The Mitchells moved into a two-story house near the state capitol, only a few blocks from the St. Charles Hotel, where William became headwaiter. The couple had a son, Johnnie, and the young family prospered. Attending a school taught by two white women, Maggie earned high grades that showed her intelligence and persistence.

In 1876, when Maggie was ten, William Mitchell disappeared. Five days later his body was found floating in the James River. He'd been robbed and murdered. With no savings, insurance, or pension, the family was destitute. Besides her two children, Elizabeth Mitchell also had to support her two younger brothers who had moved in with her.

Elizabeth turned to what she did best: laundry. She gathered baskets of dirty clothes from white families, washed and boiled them in a big black pot, hung them to dry, folded and ironed them, and then sent Maggie to deliver them and collect the money. It was a never ending, backbreaking job. Seeing how crucial money was, Maggie vowed that somehow she would earn enough to support her mother and buy her some time to rest. It was a lesson that was to remain with Maggie for the rest of her life.

Maggie managed to help her mother, attend school, and do charitable and church work. She joined the First African Baptist Church at age eleven, attending church services faithfully. On her fourteenth birthday, she also joined the Good Idea Council #16 of the Independent Order of the Sons and Daughters of St. Luke, usually referred to simply as "St. Luke's." This fraternal order helped needy black families get food, clothing, employment, and burial expense funds in return for monthly dues and a promise to help out others in their time of need.

At Maggie's graduation from school in 1883, her father, Eccles Cuthbert, came back into her life. He bought her a dress for the occasion and tried to establish a relationship with her. Her mother, however, threw out the dress and refused to let Cuthbert play any part in her daughter's life. Maggie never heard from him again.

Maggie was hired to teach the elementary grades at Valley School in Richmond, earning $35 a month. Two years later she made $42.50 a month. Her school was run-down, with tattered textbooks left over from other schools, but she felt her teaching could make a difference in her students' lives, regardless of the conditions. And the money she earned helped support her mother.

In addition to teaching, Maggie was active in the Women's Missionary and Educational Society of Virginia and in the Acme Literary Society. She also took classes in accounting and business management, and continued her charitable work with St. Luke's. She was busy and productive, with little time for romance.

Then at church Maggie met Armstead Walker, who was also a graduate of the Armstrong Normal School and who worked with his father in the brick contracting business. The two liked and respected each other and fell in love. They were married in September 1886, when Maggie was twenty-three. Maggie had to give up teaching because by nineteenth-century Virginia law, married women—black or white—were not allowed to teach.

The couple lived with Armstead's parents until they built their own house on North Third Street. Prevented from teaching, Maggie continued working with service organizations in Richmond.

Their first child was born in December 1890 after a difficult birth. He was so damaged by forceps that he was expected to die during his first night. But, the baby, named Russell Eccles Talmadge Walker, miraculously made it through that first night and succeeding nights. Maggie herself was in poor health from the ordeal, and she spent the next five months bedridden. After recovering, she returned to charitable work.

Three years later Maggie and Armstead had a second son, Armstead Mitchell Walker, who lived only seven months. About the same time, Maggie's brother Johnnie came back to Richmond from New York, where he had lived and worked. Ill with tuberculosis, Johnnie was cared for by Maggie until he died in April 1894, only three months after the death of her baby.

Following the twin tragedies, the Walkers had several years of happiness. They adopted Armstead's niece, Polly Anderson, and in 1897 had another son, Melvin Dewitt Walker.

Still active in St. Luke's, Maggie pushed the order to develop a juvenile organization to get young people involved in charitable volunteer work and to prepare them for employment. She presented her idea at the order's conference in Norfolk in 1895. The idea was adopted, and Maggie was put in charge of organizing the youth order.

Displaying her talent for organization and teaching, Maggie quickly established the Youth Department of St. Luke's. Within a year the department had more than 1,000 members. The stated purpose of the organization was to prepare black youths socially and educationally for a successful life. They were taught good manners, self-improvement, thrift, spirituality, and community responsibility.

Maggie Walker knew young people. The lessons could not be direct, but had to seem like fun. Prizes were given for good attendance at meetings, and youths flocked to participate in games, parades, and competitions. A special occasion was Sunshine Day, held in November, when the young people visited shut-ins, did other good deeds, and dressed in their best to march in a parade through Richmond. Maggie was a pioneer in lifting young people's self-esteem, although she would not have called it that. St. Luke's was not about how individuals felt about themselves, but about doing good for others in order to contribute to the welfare of the entire group.

In 1899 Maggie attended the national conference of the Order of St. Luke in West Virginia. Attendees feared that St. Luke's was finished because its adult membership had dwindled to fewer than 1,000 members nationwide. With no new members to pay dues, there would be no money to pay out benefits to the needy.

Maggie decided that something must be done to keep the order going. It was too important to be allowed to die. Perhaps she was the person to do that something. When the Grand Secretary resigned, Maggie agreed to replace him, and soon discovered what an uphill job she had taken on. The treasury contained just over $30, while debts totaled more than $400.

Maggie cut her salary to $100 a year, instead of the $300 the previous Grand Secretary had been paid. She set about increasing membership, traveling and speaking throughout the eastern states.

Membership grew, and those members continued paying dues and helping each other out with food and clothes when times were hard or tragedy struck, but Maggie felt that more was needed. She believed blacks should build factories where they could manufacture clothing, especially underwear, hats, and children's clothes. It should be priced so that the poor could afford to buy, and the manufacturing would employ workers and give them a living wage. She also favored loans for the poor, rather than handouts. Loans could help men start businesses. When they succeeded, their repayment with interest would increase the fund, making it possible to make loans to others. Students, too, should be given loans, because their future prosperity depended on education. Maggie was far-seeing and forward-thinking, grasping the idea of student loans half a century before the government did.

Maggie herself could not go everywhere to spread the message of St. Luke's. The organization needed a newspaper, she thought, to keep all the members informed of what the order was doing. Thus began the *St. Luke Herald*, printed on a press owned and operated by members of the order. In addition to news of the various branches, the *Herald* published short stories and poems written by children. This built up the children's pride as well as the newspaper's readership.

Maggie next turned her attention to insurance. St. Luke's members already received financial help for burial expenses, but more support was needed. Insurance companies were controlled by whites. Maggie wanted to keep money in the black community so that those who paid into insurance companies were the ones who benefited, as recipients of aid and as investors. She established her own insurance company, offering a $100 insurance policy without a doctor's examination. Because she so firmly believed in God and in the importance of faith, however, St. Luke's would not insure anyone who did not profess belief in the Creator.

By 1903 the Order of St. Luke was a business conglomer-
ate, with factories, stores, an insurance company, and a press. At
the age of thirty-six, Maggie began what would be her most significant achievement: establishing St. Luke's Penny Savings Bank.
Her idea, again, was that blacks should keep their money in their
own community and pool their resources to help each other.
There were other banks run by black men; hers would be the first
run by a black woman. On opening day, November 2, 1903, people poured in to make deposits. The bank stayed open until
eleven that night, and by that time it had taken in $9,434.44.
This was an astonishing amount in 1903, when a man's wool suit
cost only $2.50.

Maggie wanted everyone, especially children, to see that pennies saved could become dollars, which could pay for education,
buy property, or set up a business. Children were given little card-
board boxes to save their pennies in—often forgoing a bag of
candy they could have bought with the penny—and when the box
was full, the pennies were deposited in Maggie's bank. To earn the
pennies, children found chores to do, such as mowing lawns and
running errands. Her bank complemented the lessons she'd been
teaching all along through St. Luke's Juvenile Branch: education,
thrift, generosity, Bible study, and community service.

Financial success was important, but it was not enough. Maggie noted that blacks were not allowed to be fully participating
American citizens. Poll taxes, required of everyone, and literacy
tests, required of those whose grandparents had not voted, kept
many blacks from voting. And no women could vote, no matter
how well educated or wealthy they were. The *Herald* railed against
these obstacles to full citizenship.

Then came a test of willpower for all blacks, voters or not.
Beginning on April 20, 1904, the Passenger and Power Company,
which operated Richmond's streetcars, announced it would enforce

separate seating for blacks and whites. Blacks would be asked to move into designated areas and to give up their seats to whites if the space allotted to whites was insufficient. Any who refused could be forced at gunpoint to comply. The streetcar conductors were empowered to carry weapons.

Richmond's black citizens decided to boycott streetcars. For months they walked to work, to church, to shops and schools. The *Herald* estimated that more than eighty percent of blacks supported the boycott by walking. Those who had transportation gave rides to others. By the end of the year, the Passenger and Power Company was bankrupt. Maggie and her group had demonstrated their economic power.

The Walker family prospered, and in 1905 they purchased a two-story brick house on East Leigh Street in Richmond. The house was expanded to make room for Armstead and Maggie's children, in-laws, grandchildren, and Maggie's mother. Soon the twenty-five-room mansion was a social center of Richmond. Prominent visitors to the Walker home included Booker T. Washington, W. E. B. DuBois, Langston Hughes, and Mary McCleod Bethune.

After learning accounting through a correspondence course from Loyola University, the Walkers' son Russell worked for St. Luke's Penny Savings Bank as an accountant. Their younger son, Melvin, attended Shaw University in Raleigh.

In 1910 Virginia passed a law requiring annual inspection of banks. True Reformers' Bank, a large Richmond bank owned by blacks, was found to have made poor decisions on loans and was closed. Maggie worried about the fate of St. Luke's Penny Savings, but the bank was passed by the examiners. Another law passed that same year required banks to separate from fraternal organizations, so Maggie's bank cut its ties with the Order of St. Luke, although it kept the name. The next year, 1911, the bank moved into new, bigger quarters.

Just when things were going so well for the Walkers, when the bank was flourishing and both sons were thriving, tragedy struck.

During the summer of 1915, there were reports of a prowler in the Walkers' neighborhood. Russell bought a gun to protect the family. One night when Maggie, Russell, and a neighbor were sitting on the front porch, someone reported seeing a man walking on the Walkers' roof. Russell rushed inside, got his gun, and shot blindly at the figure on the roof. His bullet struck, and the figure fell to the ground.

It was Armstead. Russell had killed his own father! Although the coroner stated that the shooting was an accident, rumors flew and newspaper headlines accused Russell of murder. He was arrested and, after several delays, was tried and found not guilty. Maggie had lost her husband, but her son was returned to her.

Members of the Order of St. Luke demanded that Maggie resign as Grand Secretary, claiming that the killing and trial had harmed the reputation of the order. Her friends and colleagues, who should have supported her, condemned her. In her grief, the easy thing would have been to resign, but Maggie saw that she had to defend herself and her son's reputation. She stood before the conference and passionately reminded them of all she had done for the order, taking over when it was at the bottom, increasing membership, establishing banks and businesses, and working to improve the conditions for every member. In the end, the order voted to keep Maggie on as Grand Secretary.

She also continued as president of St. Luke's Penny Savings Bank, watching its deposits increase to more than $376,000 by 1919. No longer dealing in pennies, but now a substantial organization, the bank's name was changed to St. Luke's Bank and Trust.

During the 1920s, deposits declined as all Americans took on more debt, especially installment plan buying, and gambled in the stock market. Three black banks remained open in Richmond, and the managers realized that the uncertain financial climate could cause one or all of them to fail. The best plan was to pool their resources and form one solid bank. St. Luke's and Second Street Bank merged, forming Consolidated Bank and Trust Company. The new bank, run by Maggie Walker, opened for business January 2, 1930. Its main branch, located at First and Marshall Streets in Richmond, is the longest continuously operated black bank in America.

Maggie Walker continued to work for the betterment of her race and especially for black women throughout her life. A charter member of the National Association for the Advancement of Colored People, she organized the local chapter of the National Council of Colored Women. She helped establish a Community House that brought women together to learn better ways of cooking and caring for home and family, and she arranged for a visiting nurse to improve health care for black families. Remembering the death of her brother Johnnie, she supported Piedmont Tuberculosis Sanitarium for Negroes in Burkeville, Virginia, and served on its advisory board. She was also a trustee of Virginia Union University and the National Training School in Washington, D.C.

Eleanor Roosevelt wrote Maggie a letter of appreciation for all her work on behalf of her race. Maggie was given an honorary master of science degree from Virginia Union, and there was even discussion of establishing a "Maggie Walker Month" to recognize her achievements. Maggie had gone from poverty to great wealth by her own efforts, without handouts. She was one of the wealthiest, most influential businesswomen in America.

In her business, she carried out her beliefs as well, hiring women to work in the bank and seeing to it that they were paid good wages, saved their money, and bought property. Maggie's own life was an example of what a woman could accomplish, and she carried on in spite of personal problems.

Her mother, Elizabeth Draper Mitchell, who had brought Maggie up and served as a role model of what a woman could be, died in 1922. The following year Maggie's son Russell died of alcoholism and tuberculosis. He had never recovered from the tragedy of shooting his father, and alcohol had destroyed his family life and professional career.

Suffering from diabetes, Maggie was often in pain and unable to walk. Russell's daughter, Maggie Laura Walker, lived with her grandmother and cared for her, pushing Maggie's wheelchair and accompanying her to doctors' appointments and to Hot Springs, Arkansas, for treatment. An elevator was installed in the Walker house to make it easier for Maggie to attend to business, and she bought an eight-passenger 1929 Packard equipped with a ramp for her wheelchair. She continued to go to her office until two days before her death.

Maggie Lena Mitchell Walker died on December 15, 1934, of diabetic gangrene. People all across America sent condolences to Richmond, where black and white businesses alike flew flags at half-mast. Thousands called at the house on Leigh Street to pay their respects, recognizing that in losing Maggie they had lost a remarkable lady. Her funeral at First American Baptist Church was one of the largest in the city's history. She was buried in Evergreen Cemetery in Richmond, and a high school in Richmond was named in her honor.

In 1974, forty years after her death, the Maggie L. Walker Historical Foundation was established to preserve her home as a national shrine. The Walker family deeded the house to the United States National Park Service in 1979, and it is now a National Historic Site, open to the public.

EDITH BOLLING WILSON
1872–1961

Acting President

*W*hen Edith Bolling was a few months old, an aunt commented that she was the ugliest baby in the family.

Edith's mother stoutly denied the charge, adding that even if Edith weren't beautiful, she was so good-natured that no one would notice her looks. She would have a fine future.

Her mother's assessment proved more accurate than anyone could have dreamed. The "ugly baby," a descendant of Pocahontas, became First Lady of the United States and even performed the duties of the presidency during her husband's illness.

Edith's grandfather, Dr. Archibald Bolling, owned a plantation near Lynchburg, Virginia. Her father, William Bolling, attended law school but planned to return to the plantation and earn a living as a farmer. The Civil War ended that dream. Bolling's livestock were slaughtered and the fences and buildings destroyed by Union soldiers. Then high taxes were imposed on land by the Reconstruction government.

The Bolling family moved to Wytheville, in western Virginia, where Dr. Bolling's wife had inherited a house. William Bolling set up a law practice in the town.

Edith Bolling, circa 1913

The Bolling household was crowded. Edith, born in 1872, was the seventh of eleven children, two of whom died in infancy. In addition, both grandmothers lived in the household after the deaths of their husbands. Edith shared a room with Grandmother Bolling, who taught her to read, write, figure, and read French.

Edith had only two years of formal schooling. At fifteen she was sent to Martha Washington College in Abingdon, not far from Wytheville. She disliked the stern headmaster and lost weight on the austere diet. She was delighted to drop out of school and return home after a year. During the next year, a thirty-eight-year-old man began courting her. Concerned that she might marry too young, her parents sent her to school in Richmond. Edith loved it, but her father thought her three younger brothers needed an education more than she did. Because he couldn't afford to educate them all, Edith's schooldays ended when she was eighteen.

That winter, 1890, she went to Washington to visit her sister Gertrude, who had married Alexander Galt. Here she met his cousin, Norman Galt, when he came to dinner. Edith came in late from attending her first opera and had no time to dress for dinner, but she chatted enthusiastically about the opera. She was astonished that Galt was interested in her.

Norman Galt was part owner of the family jewelry store, the finest in Washington. He was twenty-seven, well dressed, courteous, and polished. He fell in love with Edith and courted her for four years before she agreed to marry him.

Two years after their marriage, Edith lost their baby, and because of complications of childbirth, was unable to have any more children. Still, they had each other, and they led an active social life.

The Galts' lives changed drastically over the next few years. Norman's father died, then Norman's brother became an invalid in their care until his death. After Edith's father died, Norman arranged for two of her brothers to come to Washington to work in Galt's jewelry store, and they sent the youngest to a good private school.

Edith and Norman prospered. Norman gave his wife an electric car, one of the first in Washington. It was handsomely outfitted; it even had a mounted silver vase to hold an orchid. In an era when women were driven about in carriages, Edith drove her electric car around the city. She was always fashionably dressed. Edith and Norman traveled twice to Europe, where Edith bought Paris fashions designed just for her.

They were planning a third trip in 1906 when Edith had appendicitis. Having a morbid fear of hospitals, she declared she'd rather die at home than enter a hospital for surgery. Norman and her doctor acceded to her wishes, and the surgery was performed on boards placed over a table in the Galts' home. Fortunately, there were no adverse effects, but Edith had a long convalescence. Soon after, Norman became ill with what was diagnosed as a liver infection. He died quickly, at age forty-five.

Edith was now sole owner of Galt's. She retained the manager who'd worked for Norman, but she checked the books regularly herself. Eventually she sold the store at a price that would keep her in luxury for life.

Having no children, Edith opened her home to Galt and Bolling family members and took relatives on trips with her. She was about to leave for Europe in 1911 when a friend died. He had asked Edith to look after his daughter, Altrude Gordon. Edith called on the orphaned teenager and impulsively invited her along on the European trip. Altrude accepted, the trip was a success, and thus began a friendship that led to Edith's meeting with President Woodrow Wilson.

It seemed that the two were fated to meet, although Edith did not encourage it. She had heard Wilson speak in 1909 at Princeton University. When he was elected president in 1912, she declined to attend his inaugural, even though her sister-in-law came to Washington expressly to witness the event.

Edith saw the president at the theater one evening, but she concentrated on the play. Her sister-in-law arranged for the two of them to tour the White House the next day and meet the president. Edith refused. She drove her guest to the White House, dropped her off, and picked her up later.

Altrude and Edith postponed a planned trip to Europe in 1914 and instead went on a rugged camping and hiking trip to Maine. War began in Europe that summer, and in the White House, the President grieved over the death of his wife, Ellen. His two older daughters were married, and his youngest was away at school. The lonely President asked his cousin Helen Bones to stay at the White House as hostess.

Altrude Gordon eventually fell in love with Cary Grayson, Woodrow Wilson's personal physician. As Altrude's guardian, Edith met the young doctor. Dr. Grayson told Edith about Helen Bones, who was lonely and knew few people in Washington. Edith and Helen were introduced, and they began taking walks together.

One day in March 1915, Helen insisted Edith come to the White House for tea after their walk. Edith demurred, protesting that her shoes were muddy from walking and not suitable for a White House visit. Helen assured her friend that they'd be alone and no one would care about her shoes. Cousin Woodrow would be out playing golf.

Only he wasn't. A sudden downpour had ended his golf game early. When the elevator doors opened to the family wing of the White House, there stood the president. He joined the ladies for tea and was immediately taken with the buxom, dark-haired Edith. He gave her a tour of the White House and by the time she left for home, the two were laughing together. Helen remarked that it was the first time she'd heard the president laugh since his wife's death.

A few days later Edith was invited to the White House for dinner, and a few days after that, for a drive in the country—with President Wilson, Helen, and the Secret Service. The dinners and drives became frequent, always concluding with long talks. They called each other Mr. President and Mrs. Galt, but they discussed their similar backgrounds, their favorite books, and their likes and dislikes. They wrote each other poetry and long, passionate letters. Wilson also made it his mission to educate Edith politically. He shared the most important government papers with her, discussed bills that had come to him for signature into law, and read her dispatches from foreign leaders.

Soon Edith was eating dinner at the White House every evening. She told the president that she was thinking of taking a long trip to the Orient.

One evening in early May, less than two months after they met, Edith dined at the White House along with Dr. Grayson, one of the president's daughters, and several other guests. After dinner, the president got Edith alone on the veranda and told her that he loved her, and that he'd confided this to his children. He needed her at his side. He begged her to give up any thoughts of going to the Orient and instead to marry him.

Edith protested that it was too soon, they'd only known each other two months, and it was less than a year since his wife had died. If he pressed her for an immediate answer, she'd have to decline. Otherwise, if he were willing to wait, she'd think it over.

She continued to see the president. In the summer, she visited the vacation house he and his family rented in New Hampshire and told him that if he were defeated in the 1916 election—more than a year away—she'd marry him. If they married sooner, it might spoil his chances for reelection.

At White House dinners she found him in worried discussion with aides about the war in Europe. Wilson sympathized with the

Allies, but he didn't want America to get involved. It was sure to result in the loss of many young American men. He agonized over his decision. He told Edith he understood her reluctance to take on the responsibilities of First Lady at such a stressful time, that he couldn't really ask it of her. She said she was volunteering for the position, accepting his proposal. The following day they announced their engagement to Wilson's daughters.

But their future together was far from smooth sailing. Wilson's enemies spread stories that Edith and the president had planned Ellen's death, abetted by Dr. Grayson; that Wilson had beaten Ellen; that he was neglecting his official duties as president because of Edith. Most damaging was the revelation of a relationship Wilson had had with a Mrs. Mary Peck years before. He'd written her many letters and given her $7,500. Reporters hinted that if he married Edith, the whole sordid story would be published.

Wilson's son-in-law William McAdoo and his adviser Edward House, attempting to break up the romance until after the 1916 election, told Wilson how embarrassing it would be for Edith if the Peck letters were published. Agreeing with them, Wilson sent Dr. Grayson to tell Edith he was releasing her from the engagement out of concern for her reputation. She wrote back that she would stand by him, not out of duty or pity, but because she loved him.

For three days she heard nothing. He must not want her, she decided. Then Grayson came to say the president was ill and needed her. She went immediately to the White House, sat down beside him, and took his hand. Talking quietly, they decided to go ahead and marry soon. Wilson confessed that he had not answered Edith's letter because he had not read it. He had not dared to open it, fearing she was agreeing to the suggested breakup.

Their engagement was announced officially, and further rumors spread—among them that Mrs. Peck had been bought off with Edith's money. Ignoring the gossip, Edith and Woodrow

Wilson were married at her home on the evening of December 18, 1915. They took the train, along with Secret Service protectors, to Hot Springs, Virginia, for a honeymoon.

Despite his advisers' concern, Wilson's marriage was not a handicap to his winning reelection. Edith proved to be a good campaigner, smiling and waving at crowds wherever the Wilsons went. Wilson campaigned on the slogan, "He kept us out of war." When the votes were counted, Wilson had won a second term, the first Democrat to do so since Andrew Jackson.

The Wilsons shared not only a bed (some presidential couples had not) but most of their waking hours as well. Edith sat in the Oval Office with her husband, decoding secret messages and acting as his unofficial secretary and adviser.

Soon, however, Wilson had to break his promise to keep America out of the conflict in Europe. He asked Congress to declare war because of continued German submarine attacks against America's ships. Edith pitched in to help in the war effort, conserving food, working in hospitals, even pasturing sheep on the White House lawn to provide wool for military clothing. Most importantly, however, she protected the president's health, persuading him to take breaks to relieve the stress of the job.

Agonizing over the horrible loss of life, Wilson wrote the Fourteen Points that he believed the Allies and the enemy must adhere to for world peace. When an armistice was agreed to in November 1918, he and Edith sailed for Europe to attend the peace conference. Wilson was the first American president to leave the country while in office.

The president and his wife were greeted with parties, parades, and presentations to royalty. One noblewoman curtsied before Edith, having heard that she was descended from a princess. Wilson was excited about his Fourteen Points and how they might change the world. Alas, the other Allies, determined to punish

Germany, defeated one provision after another of his proposal, and the Germans were angry that they had surrendered on his promise of fair treatment. Wilson worked and argued until he fell ill. He grew thin and stooped, aging before Edith's eyes. Finally, the ancient rivalries of Europe were too much. Everything had been compromised or ruined outright except Point 14, the League of Nations.

The Wilsons sailed home to persuade Congress to agree to the treaty, and after only ten days, sailed back to Europe. Then Wilson discovered that his assistant, Colonel Edward House, had gutted the League provision. Stunned, Wilson returned to the States, determined to take his case to the American people. Only through international cooperation could the nations of the world avoid further wars, he said.

On September 3, 1919, the Wilsons left for a train trip to visit all but four of the states west of the Mississippi. Accompanying them were Dr. Grayson, their personal servants, and an army of reporters and Secret Service personnel. It was a tightly scheduled trip. Edith feared there would be no time for much-needed rest.

All went well for a while. Crowds welcomed them, cheering for the president and his beautifully dressed First Lady. At each stop he made speeches urging the importance of the League of Nations, and smiled and shook the hands of thousands of Americans. After each event, he complained of dreadful headaches. Meanwhile, back in Washington, Congressional enemies were speaking against the League.

In California, Edith invited the infamous Mrs. Peck for lunch with her and the president. Mrs. Peck said reporters had searched her house for the president's letters. Wilson offered her financial help, but she declined.

The presidential party headed east. The weather was hot, and Wilson's headaches worsened. He couldn't eat or sleep, his face twitched, and he sweated profusely. Edith begged him to take a few days off, but he refused. In the night, as the train approached Wichita, he had Edith send for Dr. Grayson. His left arm and leg were paralyzed by a stroke. Still he insisted the trip must go on, and Edith had to tell him the public must not see him as he was.

Dr. Grayson canceled the remainder of the trip and had the train head back to Washington immediately. He gave reporters a statement blaming the president's illness on a recurrence of influenza. Wilson managed to walk from the train to the White House car, and later, to sign a few bills.

Then, on October I, the president collapsed in the bathroom. Doctors kept everyone away except Edith, and rumors flew that Wilson was dead. Vice President Thomas Marshall was told that the president could die at any moment.

Dr. Grayson was also a military officer, sworn to support his Commander-in-Chief. He could not bring himself to declare Wilson incompetent. But the government must go on. Edith took charge, announcing to the public that Wilson was still president, that he was recovering and would be able to carry on his official functions, but that he could not receive visitors. Letters and congressional bills piled up. Some were taken to the president, who signed them shakily, his hand guided by Edith's.

Edith kept congressmen and members of the cabinet from seeing the president. Many of them had opposed the president on the League of Nations. Angry senators proposed amendments to the League of Nations proposal, but Wilson insisted there be no compromise. Nor would the Senate compromise. The treaty was defeated.

Edith took charge of all incoming mail. She sent back notations of what the president wanted or had said, initialed by her. When officials demanded to see the president, she refused. Official business could wait. Her job was to get him well. Newspapers and influential people began to refer to her as the "Presidentress" and declared that America had a woman president when most women could not even vote.

When a crisis arose with Mexico, Senator Albert Fall asked to see the president urgently. If refused, Fall planned to begin impeachment proceedings. Edith and Dr. Grayson agreed to the visit, and amazingly, Wilson was able to talk with the senator from his bed.

The cabinet continued meeting without the president. Two cabinet secretaries resigned, and Edith appointed their successors, saying she was acting on the president's wishes.

Gradually Wilson got better. He walked in the White House with the help of aides. Edith was always at his side, encouraging him and keeping critics away.

As the election of 1920 approached, Edith and Grayson were appalled to realize that Wilson wanted to run again! Working in secret, they persuaded the convention delegates not to nominate him.

The Democrats lost badly to Harding. On March 4, 1921, Wilson was lifted into an open car beside Harding for his final ride to the Capitol. He signed a few papers, dismissed Congress, and left with Edith for S Street, where they had bought a house with the financial help of ten friends.

Edith had kept her husband in the presidency until the end, opposing those who wanted him to resign. For eighteen months she had been more than his helper and mainstay. She had made government decisions, signed bills into law, and appointed officers.

Letters poured in for the former president: requests for his opinion or for his attendance at various functions, offers for his writing. He rejected them all. He became a partner in a law firm, but resigned when he discovered only the prestige of his name was wanted. He typed the first page of his autobiography, a loving dedication to Edith. People sent gifts and letters.

On November 11, 1921, the Wilsons attended the dedication of the Tomb of the Unknown Soldier at Arlington. Afterward, cheering crowds followed the Wilsons back to S Street. They came again on Armistice Day 1923, after he'd made a short radio speech.

In late January 1924, Dr. Grayson left for Florida. Edith sent for him four days later. She knew her beloved Woodrow so well that she could tell the end was near. His children were summoned, and the press gathered outside the Wilsons' house. His last spoken word was "Edith!" as she sat holding his hand. He died on February 3, 1924.

Edith went into seclusion for a year, spending most of her time answering more than 8,000 telegrams and letters of sympathy. She was aided by her brother, Randolph Bolling, who had also been her husband's secretary after he left the White House.

Edith refused to make speeches or to campaign for any politicians. She traveled, and wherever she went, she was honored as the widow of the great Woodrow Wilson. She stayed in castles and palaces as the guest of foreign rulers. In 1929 she made a trip around the world.

Mainly, however, Edith dedicated herself to keeping alive the ideals and memory of Woodrow Wilson. Various Wilson aides, including Colonel House, wrote their memoirs, but because Edith found them unfair to Wilson, she wrote her own memoir of the Wilson presidential years. Although she didn't intend to publish it, her friend Bernard Baruch persuaded her to do so. It was the first memoir written by an American president's wife. She gave the money she received from its sale to her brother Randolph. When a film was made of her husband's life in 1946, she donated the $50,000 she received to the Woodrow Wilson Foundation. The Foundation made Wilson's birthplace in Staunton, Virginia, into a national shrine and provided scholarships to students who studied and followed his ideals.

Edith lived on in the house on S Street for more than thirty-five years. One of the last official events she attended was the Presidential Inaugural in 1961. The day she died, December 28, 1961, she had been scheduled to attend the opening of the Woodrow Wilson Bridge over the Potomac River. She was eighty-nine. She is buried beside her husband in the National Cathedral in Washington, D.C.

ELLEN GLASGOW
1873–1945

Prize-Winning Author

$\mathcal{E}$agerly, Ellen Glasgow awaited the publication of the Pulitzer Prizes. Her novel, *The Sheltered Life*, had been nominated as the best fiction of 1932. This was to be her vindication to those who said her writing was uneven and sometimes too sentimental.

But when the list was published, she saw that she hadn't won. This latest loss was almost too much to bear. She'd lost family, the man she loved, much of her hearing, and now the Pulitzer yet again. Why keep on writing? She sank into depression and for a time withdrew even further from life around her.

Eventually she realized that she had to go on writing. Writing was her life. And she would triumph, she vowed. She would win the Pulitzer Prize.

Ellen Anderson Glasgow was born in Richmond, Virginia, in 1873, to a family more prosperous than many of their neighbors in the post–Civil War South. Her father, Francis Glasgow, was the managing director of Tredegar Iron Works, where he had been employed since 1849. The iron works, which had provided cannon and armaments for the Confederacy during the war, turned afterward to producing rails and other industrial goods for rebuilding.

Ellen Glasgow

Although Francis Glasgow was a good financial provider for his growing family, he was a stern Scotch-Irish Presbyterian and an unaffectionate father.

Ellen's parents were opposites. Her mother, Anne Glasgow, was the gentle descendant of a Cavalier family of Tidewater, Virginia, and an Episcopalian. Twenty-one at the time of her marriage, Anne eventually bore ten children. Ellen was the eighth. She always felt torn between the personalities and beliefs of her parents.

When Ellen was two, she contracted diphtheria. Her mother had just given birth to a new baby, so she was unavailable to be with Ellen during her illness. The diphtheria may have led to Ellen's later hearing loss.

As economic conditions improved in Virginia, Francis Glasgow bought a plantation called Jerdone Castle, where the family spent their summers, and a larger house in Richmond on Main Street. Ellen loved the farm and spent hours talking to the former slaves who worked the land as tenants, did laundry for her family, cooked, and cared for the children. They shared stories and songs with her.

At age three she invented stories about the adventures of a character she called Willie. Willie remained with her until she began to read Dickens at age twelve and discovered a wealth of characters more interesting than her make-believe friend.

Ellen loved words and decided at seven to become a writer, jotting down verses about life on the farm. Her father read aloud to the family every night and discussed what he'd read with the children, so Ellen knew English literature and English history well, but was woefully ignorant of geography or arithmetic. When she was sent to school, she lasted less than a day. She was put in the lowest class even though she could read and write and was humiliated when she couldn't do the simplest arithmetic problem. Further, an older student conned Ellen out of her lunch. She developed a nervous headache and ran home from school. Her mother sympathetically sent for a doctor, who recommended a long rest before Ellen could attend school again.

Anne Glasgow suffered from what would now be called manic depression or bipolar disorder. She was alternately cheerful and morbid, and her children were unable to cope or understand her moodiness and despair. Because Anne hated Jerdone Castle, Francis sold the farm, and the family moved permanently to the city. Ellen, then age ten, was torn from the surroundings she loved and forced to leave behind her pet dog.

Like many other young Virginia women, Ellen was expected to "come out" socially. When she was sixteen, she spent part of the winter in Charleston, South Carolina, where she attended the St. Cecilia Ball. Later that same year she was invited to social functions at the University of Virginia. She was pretty and liked attention, but she was painfully shy. She also seemed to have difficulty hearing what people said to her and feared she might be going deaf.

Ellen's sister Cary and her husband Walter McCormack gave Ellen a subscription to the Mercantile Library of New York. Books then were not merely checked out of libraries but had to be rented. The McCormacks couldn't have found a better gift for Ellen. Parcels of books arrived regularly at the Glasgow home in Richmond. Ellen read Darwin and the economist Henry George; influenced by their ideas, she briefly became a socialist and joined the reformist group, the Fabian Society. She had no further formal schooling.

She also worked as a volunteer at the Sheltering Arms Hospital in Richmond. Since her family supported her, she had no need of paid employment. At the hospital, she was appalled by the squalor, by the poor who did little to help themselves, and by the social structure that allowed such poverty to exist. Her writing would later reflect all these experiences.

By reading widely, Ellen was able to pass an exam on political economy at the University of Virginia. Because she was a woman, she could be tutored but could not attend classes at the University, an exclusion she resented bitterly.

Writing secretly with no encouragement from her family, Ellen at eighteen completed a four-hundred-page novel, *Sharp Realities*, which she sent to a literary critic along with the fifty-dollar fee her sister Cary had given her.

Soon after, Ellen went with a group of young ladies to New York City. While others were seeing the sights, Ellen went on two secret missions. She consulted an ear specialist, who told her she was not going deaf. She also slipped away from the group to meet with the literary critic.

When she asked his opinion of her manuscript, she discovered it had not been opened. The critic was only interested in her as a sexual conquest, not as a writer. He pulled her into his arms and tried to kiss her. Horrified and angry, she escaped and paid a messenger to retrieve her manuscript the next day. On her return home she burned her book and resolved to give up writing. Soon, however, she began writing *The Descendant*, which was influenced by the ideas of Henry George. In it she criticized the pretenses of the Southern way of life.

When Ellen was twenty, her mother died of typhoid after only a week's illness. Ellen was devastated and became ill herself, suffering from severe headaches. Again she gave up writing. What was the point? Life was unfair. She destroyed most of *The Descendant*, but two years later rewrote it from memory.

Securing a letter of introduction from a friend for the chief reader at Macmillan, she mailed him the manuscript and then went again to New York. He took her to lunch at Delmonico's and told her that no young woman should write novels; she should go home and have babies. Another setback. Ellen stayed in New York six weeks and arranged for an interview at University Publishing Company, with a letter of recommendation from Dr. G. F. Holmes, the professor at the University of Virginia who had administered her political economy exam. The head of the firm told her he was impressed with her writing but that his firm only published textbooks. He turned her manuscript over to an employee, a Mr. Patton. Patton called on her the next day, said he'd stayed awake all night reading it, and assured her that it would be published.

Ellen's brother Arthur, who was living in England, invited her to visit. To make certain she wouldn't refuse, he bought a ticket on a ship and even clothes for her. She thought the timing was wrong but went anyway. She had begun having headaches again and had a case of the flu.

A letter from Patton told her he had sent her manuscript to Century Publishing and that they would publish it if she would make a few changes in the first six chapters. She did and sent it back. He submitted it instead to Harper and Row. Ellen went to Paris, where a telegram from Patton told her of the publication of *The Descendant* in 1896. Her name was not on the title page; it was published anonymously. But still, it was published!

Her joy was somewhat subdued by her growing deafness. On her return to New York that autumn, another ear specialist confirmed her fear: She was indeed losing her hearing.

Ellen began writing another book. She wrote realistic stories, hating the romances popular at the time and being disgusted with the romanticism of the post–Civil War South. Such writing to her was escapism, looking back at an idealistic South and refusing to deal with the problems of the present. She broke with the popular tradition of Southern writers. Her book dealt with a poor farmer and with illegitimacy. Traditionally Southern books had been written about owners of large plantations. Southern women then were not expected to write novels or even to know about illicit sex.

Always a voracious reader, she read everything she could. From Henry James she learned the technical aspects of the novel—

her literary rebellion and that of other writers had brought about nothing but the ability to use vulgarisms in novels. Perhaps the Southern gentility she had despised was not so bad.

Though Ellen felt she had accomplished little, the importance of her work was being recognized. The University of North Carolina, the University of Richmond, Duke University, and the College of William and Mary all awarded her honorary degrees, and in 1940 she received the Howells Medal for distinguished work in literature, given by the American Academy of Arts and Letters. She had produced twenty novels, but the big prize, the Pulitzer, eluded her.

Her heart condition grew worse in the summer of 1940, and she feared she would die soon. She had written the second draft of her next novel, *In This Our Life*, and did not feel she could complete the third. This time instead of typing a third version, she corrected directly onto the pages with the help of friend and fellow writer, James Branch Cabell, and submitted the manuscript for publication.

On May 4, 1942, when her country was again at war, she received a telephone call from Donald Brace, co-founder of Harcourt, Brace and Company, now her publishers. *In This Our Life* had won the Pulitzer Prize for fiction for the year.

Prize-winning author Ellen Glasgow died three years later on November 21, 1945, and is buried in Richmond, Virginia.

NANCY LANGHORNE ASTOR

1879–1964

Member of Parliament

$\mathcal{N}$ancy Astor assured her husband, Waldorf, that he could win election to Parliament from the city of Plymouth, England. Never mind that it was a Liberal stronghold and he represented the Conservative party. Waldorf had Liberal tendencies, unusual in someone who had inherited one of the largest fortunes in the world. Waldorf and Nancy would campaign, she told him, and they would buy a house in Plymouth and get to know the people there, even though living in one's district was not required in Britain.

Throughout 1909 Nancy went door to door in Plymouth, describing her husband's program and urging the residents to vote for him. Waldorf campaigned when he could, but his health was poor, and he collapsed from exhaustion shortly before the election. He lost by only 500 votes out of 15,000 cast.

Waldorf was deeply disappointed, but the Conservatives considered it a victory, as it had been a long-shot election. Next time Waldorf would win, Nancy said confidently, and set about planning his next campaign. Less than a year later he did win, becoming one of the youngest members of Parliament. He and Nancy

Nancy Langhorne Astor, 1928

were just thirty-one years old—both sharing a May 19 birthday—and the whole world seemed open to them and their ideas.

Nancy Astor had come a long way from her birthplace in Danville, Virginia, in 1879.

Nancy was the eighth child of eleven born to Nancy ("Nanaire") and Chiswell ("Chillie") Langhorne. Both parents came from good families, but like nearly everyone else in Virginia after the Civil War, they were impoverished. Everything their families had owned beforehand had been destroyed.

Chillie supported the family as a tobacco auctioneer until he was given an opportunity in railroad building. He moved the family to Richmond, and after the small railroad job was completed, he again worked as an auctioneer until he met a former Union officer whom he'd known during the Civil War. Although Chillie had fought for the Confederacy, he was well liked by his enemies as well. The Union officer saw to it that Chillie received the government contract for railroad building in Virginia.

This time Chillie made a fortune. He bought a grand house in Richmond and an even grander mansion and plantation, Mirador, near Charlottesville. Here Nancy grew up in elegant surroundings. The eldest Langhorne daughter, Lizzie, had married in Richmond while the family was still poor. The next, Irene, made her debut, and was eloquently described by newspapers. In New York she attracted the attention of Charles Dana Gibson, famous society painter and creator of the Gibson Girl image. Irene personified the image. The two were married and traveled widely.

Nancy also went north to a finishing school, where she amused and shocked her classmates with her daring pranks and vivacious manner. She even made up stories about her family and exaggerated her Southern accent to entertain the students. She hated the school, however, and was eventually allowed to come home to Virginia.

Back at Mirador, she met the new Episcopal clergyman, Reverend Frederick Neve, who was to influence her life more than anyone other than her parents. Reverend Neve, who became her friend for life, took the impressionable young woman along with others to visit the poor and distribute food. These visits opened Nancy's eyes to poverty. She enjoyed visiting the elderly, entertaining them with stories and jokes. Her quick wit and vitality were to be her biggest assets for the rest of her life.

Nancy lacked Irene's classic beauty, but she had a small, lithe body, glossy brown hair, and a fine-featured, "interesting" face. She rode well, a quality prized both in Virginia and in England.

As a relatively uneducated Southern girl, she was expected to marry well, not to have a career. Irene had found her wealthy husband in the North, so perhaps Nancy could also, Chillie and Nanaire decided. She was sent to visit the Gibsons at Newport, where she attracted the attention of Robert Gould Shaw.

From a wealthy and distinguished Boston family, Shaw was intrigued with the outspoken Virginian, and almost immediately proposed. Nancy accepted, and the two were married at Mirador in 1897.

Nancy rushed back to Mirador soon after the honeymoon, confessing to her parents that she'd made a dreadful mistake. The marriage was over, as far as she was concerned. She was already pregnant, however, and both families urged Nancy and Robert to stay married. Chillie bought them a house in Virginia where they and their son Bobby lived together for three more years. Shaw became an alcoholic, and the couple separated. Although Nancy opposed divorce, she finally consented to sign divorce papers in February 1903 when the Shaws told her Robert had already married someone else and would be charged with bigamy unless she freed him. Divorce was rare then, and divorced women were often ostracized.

To cheer Nancy up, her mother took her and a friend to

Europe for several months. Soon after their return to Virginia, Nanaire died suddenly, and Nancy spent the next year supervising the running of Mirador and trying to manage her irrepressible father. Chillie suggested she go to Europe again, and in late 1904 she did, accompanied by her son Bobby, her sister Phyllis, and Phyllis's two children. Nancy liked England, but many of the Englishmen she might have been interested in marrying were taken aback by her outspoken ways. The group returned to Mirador in the spring of 1905. A friend of her brother's courted Nancy, with Chillie's encouragement, but she wasn't interested.

Nancy's life took an exciting turn in December 1905 when she and Chillie sailed for London on the same ship as Waldorf Astor. Born in America, Astor had immigrated to England with his father, Lord William Waldorf Astor, who had purchased Hever Castle and Cliveden estate, as well as an interest in businesses and a newspaper in England. It was rumored that Chillie had found out which ship Waldorf was scheduled to sail on and planned the meeting.

Waldorf was captivated with Nancy. He didn't care what his English neighbors thought of her, but the fact that Nancy was divorced caused problems for the couple. Several clergymen refused to marry them. Finally, they wed quietly in London in April 1906. Chillie was delighted at the marriage.

Lord Astor met his daughter-in-law soon after the ceremony, and, as many men before and afterward, he was charmed by Nancy. For a wedding gift, he gave the young couple Cliveden, the vast mansion built in the 1600s by the Duke of Buckingham. He moved into smaller Hever Castle.

In July of that year, Nancy and Waldorf visited Mirador. They attended parties there and in Lynchburg, then the whole Langhorne family went to the Gibsons' summer place in Maine, taking along a retinue of servants to care for them. Nancy was eager to leave America. Much as she loved Virginia, she knew that her life now was in England. The Astors returned to Cliveden in the autumn.

Nancy set about changing Cliveden, getting rid of some of the dark, stuffy furnishings and brightening up the place. While Waldorf dealt with financial issues and breeding horses, Nancy supervised a staff of more than a hundred, including a personal secretary, a personal maid, and a housekeeper. Well organized, she had a list brought to her each morning of the sick who needed attending, tasks that must be completed, and any social events to plan or attend.

Writers George Bernard Shaw and Hilary Belloc were frequent Astor guests over decades, and T. E. Lawrence was a special friend. Soon an invitation to Cliveden was coveted. English society had accepted Nancy in spite of her divorced status and foreign birth. Cliveden also became headquarters for visiting Langhornes, especially Nancy's sisters, Phyllis and Nora.

Another visitor to Cliveden was Winston Churchill. Nancy found him imaginative, but the two disagreed on so many issues that their antagonism became legendary.

William, the first of the Astors' five children, was born in 1907. Nancy was expecting their second, a daughter, in 1909 when Waldorf decided to stand for election to Parliament. She campaigned for him, and when he was stricken with tuberculosis, she accompanied him to a sanatorium in Scotland, sleeping outside in the cold alongside him. Nancy and Waldorf were temperamental opposites—she vivacious and quick-tempered, he patient and shy—but they were devoted to each other and thought alike on many issues, including what they could do to better the world with his tremendous fortune.

Waldorf voted against his party in favor of Prime Minister Lloyd George's budget and again for George's social insurance bill that for the first time provided welfare benefits to poor English fam-

ilies. Waldorf worked on various health committees and bought the
Observer, keeping on as editor the liberal Irishman J. L. Garvin. The
Astors were thus exposed to the point of view from this man of dif-
ferent social class, and they enjoyed discussing politics with him.

After the birth of her third child, David, in 1912, Nancy was
in poor health. Her weakness irritated her. Her father had never
been sick, and neither should she be, she thought. The Astors and
their friends made a skiing trip to St. Moritz, which took away her
depression, but doctors prescribed more rest.

Nancy was diagnosed with "internal abscesses" and had surgery. She recuperated at the Astors' vacation cottage in Sandwich,
where she heard about Christian Scientist teacher Mary Baker
Eddy and sent for her. Nancy became a follower of that faith, and
she made a full recovery.

World War I brought other changes in the Astors' lives. Waldorf built a military canteen at Plymouth and offered Cliveden as
a hospital. Both Canadian and American troops were cared for
there. Nancy visited the wounded daily, scolding some, praising
others, joking with them all, hoping to hasten their recovery. During the war she gave birth to two more sons, Michael and Jacob.

Waldorf was reelected to Parliament in 1918, but the following year, his father, Lord William Waldorf Astor, died. Waldorf
inherited the title and was thus able to join the House of Lords,
leaving his Parliamentary seat vacant. There was speculation that his
younger brother would be chosen to fill the seat in the next election.

Instead, the Plymouth Sutton Conservative Association asked
Nancy to run. She was well known to the voters there, and women
had recently been given the right to vote and to stand for Parliament.
She accepted the nomination, immediately sparking controversy. Critics said she should be home looking after her children. Her response
was that her children were well-looked-after and that someone should
be in Parliament looking out for Britain's less fortunate children.

Although three candidates quickly opposed her, Nancy had the endorsement of Lloyd George and the financial and political support of Waldorf, who helped her write speeches. Using her novelty as a woman candidate to her advantage, she ran on her own personality, joking with the voters and promising not to make long speeches or to follow a specific program, but to represent her district and especially to look out for the concerns of women. One opposing candidate withdrew, and when the votes were counted, Nancy had almost as many as the two remaining candidates combined. A Virginian had just become the first woman elected to the British Parliament.

Nancy soon found listening to speeches in Parliament quite boring. Then in February 1920 she made her first speech, on the ills of alcoholism. During the war, the Liquor Control Board had restricted the sale of alcohol. Now it was proposed that the board be abolished. Because alcoholism had wrecked the lives of her brothers and of her first husband, Nancy never drank, and never served alcohol at Cliveden. She knew that alcoholism was even more devastating to families with little money, and she spoke fervently in favor of keeping the board in place. The board stayed, mainly because the government had already decided to amend rather than abolish it. Nancy, however, had made a name for herself. Her manner of speaking in Parliament—interrupting other speakers, interrupting herself to shout at other members—made her a joke to some and a nuisance to others.

Nancy's past came back to haunt her in the next issue she tackled. She opposed a bill to liberalize divorce in Britain, and angry critics pointed out that she wanted to deny to others what she had procured for herself. In fact, Nancy had opposed her own divorce on religious grounds. The only reason she had agreed to it was to protect her former husband from a charge of bigamy. This issue almost ended her political career, but she again talked her way out of trouble with the voters.

Liquor control came up for a vote again, and critics charged that Nancy wanted to impose prohibition on Britain as America had just done. Secretly she probably would have liked to do that, but publicly, she introduced a bill to prohibit the sale of alcohol to anyone younger than eighteen.

In 1922 Nancy was invited to address the League of Women Voters in Baltimore, and her visit to America became a triumphal tour, especially at her birthplace, Danville, Virginia, as people flocked to see and hear her. She had become the most famous woman in the world, with outspoken opinions on everything. Soon after her return to England, Nancy published an account of her trip called *My Two Countries*. A book reviewer used the occasion to bring up the matter of her divorce once more, and the newspaper appeared to be provoking a libel suit. A reader investigated the circumstances of the divorce and found them as Nancy had stated. The Astors decided not to sue for libel, but let the matter drop. Nancy was reelected in 1923, but by a lesser margin.

Waldorf commissioned a painting of Nancy's introduction to Parliament, escorted by Lloyd George and Lord Arthur Balfour, and presented it to the House of Commons. It caused much controversy because it appeared that Nancy was being elevated to royalty, and eventually it was withdrawn and loaned to the University of Virginia.

Nancy spoke out in favor of the League of Nations, hoping that America and Britain could cooperate with other members of the League, but America never joined. Although she became more closely identified with the Conservative Party, when the Conservatives won a landslide election, another woman was chosen as the first woman cabinet officer.

In 1931 Nancy and Waldorf made a trip that almost ended their political careers. George Bernard Shaw, always a socialist, had been invited to Russia. His wife was unable to go, so he invited the Astors and a group of friends to accompany him. Both Astors were courteous to Stalin and other Russian officials, but disturbed by what they saw. Shaw, however, began to crow about how wonderful Russian socialism was. The Astors were roundly criticized for the trip, especially by Winston Churchill. Only the collapse of the economy in 1931 took attention off their unfortunate visit.

The next controversy arose because Nancy stated that reparations against Germany had been too harsh and that the country should be treated as an equal and granted concessions that might guarantee peace. Churchill felt that the only way to stop Hitler was by going to war. The Astors thought war would bring the end of the British empire. Both sides were right.

Newspaper headlines accused the "Cliveden Set" of being pro-Nazi and the British upper class feared that socialism would spell the demise of their huge estates and privilege. Nancy struck back, writing editorials stating that she was neither a socialist nor a Nazi, but that she wanted peace and democracy. Very soon she saw that appeasement, or peace at any price, had failed, when bombs began to fall on England. Plymouth, an important naval base, was attacked in 1941, and the Astors' house there was bombed. Nancy and Waldorf both threw themselves into war work and again turned Cliveden over to the government to be used as a hospital. After the bombings, Nancy went out to comfort the bereaved and help find them shelter. She was made an honorary Private First Class.

When the war ended, Nancy and Waldorf were both sixty-six, and Waldorf was tired of politics. Realizing that there would be a huge change in the government as a result of the war, he urged Nancy not to run for reelection. After arguing with him about it, she finally consented, and on her last day in Parliament she thanked the members for accepting a foreigner into their midst even though she had fought against many of the things they stood for.

Nancy was at loose ends. Her children no longer needed her, her career was over, lifelong friends were dying, and everything was changing. Mirador was sold, and of all her sisters, only Irene remained. In the summer of 1950, Waldorf had a stroke and withdrew further from public life, but he and Nancy grew closer. He died in 1952, closing the most important relationship of her life. Nancy turned Cliveden over to her son Bill and moved into a London flat.

Growing senility—or perhaps Alzheimer's disease—kept Nancy away from mainstream events. While on a visit to her daughter in early 1964, she had a stroke and died on May 2, calling for Waldorf in her last words. She is buried beside him in Plymouth.

ANNE SPENCER
1882–1975

Poet and Activist

$\mathcal{A}$nne and Edward Spencer had been active for years in trying to establish a Lynchburg chapter of the National Association for the Advancement of Colored People (NAACP). When they were told in 1919 that the national group would send a Mr. Johnson, the chapter secretary, to Lynchburg, the Spencers offered to have the organizer stay at their home at 1313 Pierce Street.

Then Edward came down with pneumonia and Anne decided they couldn't have a guest at the time. Edward insisted that Mr. Johnson should come as planned.

He did. The "Mr. Johnson" was James Weldon Johnson, who had been American consul to Venezuela and later to Nicaragua. He had published his autobiography and volumes of poetry, and was one of the leaders of what became known as the Harlem Renaissance, an awakening of interest in African-American culture and art.

The visit was a turning point in Anne's life. She had been writing poetry most of her adult life, but it had not been published. While Johnson was visiting in Lynchburg, he read some of Anne's poems, realized how talented she was, and submitted several to H. L. Mencken, one of the most influential publishers of the

Anne and Edward Spencer
with their two daughters, Bethel and Alroy

early twentieth century. Mencken rejected her work, but offered Anne valuable criticism. Johnson then sent her work to other publishers, who accepted it.

Without Johnson's influence, Anne's poetry might never have been published. It was also Johnson's suggestion that she should be known as Anne instead of Annie.

Anne was born Annie Bethel Bannister on February 6, 1882, in Henry County, Virginia. Her father, Joel Cephus Bannister, was of mixed race—Native American, white, and black—who was born a slave in 1862. Her mother, Sarah Louise Scales Bannister, was born in 1866. She too was of mixed parentage, the daughter of a slave woman and slave owner, an aristocratic white man. Sarah was only fifteen when she married and only sixteen when her daughter Annie was born.

The Bannisters were, as Annie later wrote, too much alike in stubbornness. Joel, who ran a saloon, would take his little daughter to stand on the bar and perform for the customers. When Annie was four, Sarah decided to put a stop to this practice and went to the saloon to protest. Joel, angry at her challenging him, turned her up and spanked her before the customers. She never forgave him, and soon after took Annie away. They went first to stay with friends in North Carolina for a year and later to Bramwell, West Virginia, where Sarah got a job cooking for coal miners. Joel remained for a time in Martinsville, then moved to Illinois to work for the railroad.

The free public schools in Bramwell were for the miners' children, but Sarah wanted a better education for her daughter. Her solution was to place Annie with an educated black family. William Dixie, a barber, lived with his wife sin a substantial house and led the kind of life Sarah wanted for her daughter. Sarah saw Annie on weekends and spent most of her wages on fine clothes to complement her daughter's beauty.

Annie got along well with the Dixies and made friends among the black and white citizens in Bramwell. There were few children her own age, black or white, and she had much time to think. An intelligent girl, she soon learned to read. From the barbershop, William Dixie brought home newspapers, magazines, and well-worn books—the sentimental or lurid dime novels of the period—so Annie had a somewhat unusual reading background.

When Annie was eleven, Joel discovered that his daughter had never attended school. He wrote Sarah, telling her that if she didn't enroll Annie in school immediately, he would come and take his daughter away. Shaken, Sarah took Annie to Lynchburg, Virginia, to enroll in the Lynchburg Baptist Seminary, known later as the Virginia Theological Seminary and College and now Virginia University of Lynchburg.

Even though the minimum age for students was twelve, Sarah persuaded the principal to accept her eleven-year-old daughter. The cost was eight dollars per month. Sarah wrote to Joel, who sent ten dollars a month. He too wanted what was best for his daughter.

At the seminary, realizing how far behind other students she was, Annie spent a great deal of her time studying to catch up. To graduate, she had to take three years of Latin, one year of French, and a year of German, in addition to English, mathematics, and science. She was good at languages, writing, and literature, but poor in science. She asked a fellow student, Edward Spencer, to tutor her in the subject. In return, she would help him with Latin.

Edward, who was six years older than Annie, was unfailingly polite and pleasant. The seminary had no indoor plumbing then, and Edward would pump bath water for several girls, always including Annie. Aside from this courtesy and their studying together, the remainder of Edward's courting was done in the parlor of the seminary, under the eagle eye of chaperones.

The summer Annie was fifteen, some seminary friends invited her to visit them in Farmville. There she met the noted writer and activist W. E. B. DuBois, who was making a speaking trip throughout the South. Annie was thrilled to be introduced to the revolutionary DuBois. He was later to visit the Spencers in Lynchburg.

The valedictorian of Annie's graduating class was a poor writer, and the salutatorian was a poor speaker, so the school principal asked Annie to write and deliver the graduation speech. She always felt bad that her name was listed first in the program, rather than the two who had earned the highest grades. She quoted Alexis de Toqueville and other writers in what she later called a "black power" speech, well before the term became popular.

Virginia Seminary had no suitable auditorium for the ceremony, so the group of graduates, the faculty, and the administration took the train to Lexington, where the ceremony was held at Diamond Hill Baptist Church. Neither of Annie's parents attended the graduation. Sarah was ill; Joel sent his congratulations and began to give Annie $20 a month.

Annie spent the summer after graduation in Bramwell. She applied for a teaching job, which meant having to take an exam and attend a teachers' workshop. She was hired to teach at a school near Bramwell for $45 a month. On weekends she visited her mother and the Dixies. The following summer, she accepted an invitation to teach at Virginia Seminary.

Edward, who had gone to work in the buffet car of the New York to Montreal train, corresponded regularly with Annie. They missed each other and realized they wanted to marry.

Sarah, however, wished Annie would marry a teacher at a nearby school. She felt Annie was throwing herself away on that "porter boy" who was of a lower class and darker-skinned than she was. Sarah invited the teacher to call, but Annie fled to her room upstairs. When Sarah summoned her down, she escaped by jumping out of the window, spraining both ankles and screaming in pain; there was no pretending she might be interested in the teacher.

At this, Sarah relented. Annie and Edward were married in Bramwell on May 15, 1901. They moved to Lynchburg.

The Spencers had two daughters, Bethel and Alroy, and a son who died of diphtheria within a few hours of his birth. Their second son, Chauncey, was born after the family moved to 1313 Pierce Street, where Annie lived the rest of her life. The house was small, but over the years Edward added rooms and a second story.

Edward owned a small grocery store and then got a job with the post office delivering mail, which paid $1,000 a year, an amazing salary in 1910. He began investing in real estate, buying up small building lots for $25 or less. An enterprising man, he saw a use for discarded building materials, furniture, and other items. He brought these things home and restored them to beauty and usefulness. One visitor remarked that the rooms in the Spencers' house were all decorated differently. Annie said she wasn't surprised, as they all came from different dismantled houses.

Edward and Annie shared a love of gardening. He laid out her extensive garden behind their Pierce Street house, which soon became a Lynchburg showplace. He helped Annie tend the garden, taking her wherever she wanted to go in search of rare plants.

Edward also built Annie a garden house where she could be alone to write. He named it Edankraal, a combination of the first letters of their names, Ed and An, and the South African word *kraal*, meaning "a dwelling."

Annie led an unusual life for any woman of the early twentieth century and especially for a black middle-class woman. She did little housework. The Spencers hired someone to cook, clean, and do laundry. Annie worked in her garden, cared for the children, and wrote poetry, often living on a different schedule than her family, working in the garden by moonlight and sleeping until noon. She also taught one term without pay at Virginia Seminary when the school needed a teacher to cover an emergency vacancy.

Long before the civil rights movement of the 1960s, Annie was fighting segregation in Lynchburg. She campaigned successfully to have white teachers removed from all-black Jackson High School. Blacks were not allowed to teach at the white high school, she argued, and were thus cut off from employment in Lynchburg. She also boycotted segregated transportation. Sometimes she walked miles to avoid taking a streetcar; other times she rode on delivery wagons. Occasionally she boarded a streetcar and defiantly sat in seats reserved for whites only. It was part of her demeanor, and her reputation in Lynchburg was such that she was seldom challenged in whatever she did.

Then James Weldon Johnson came to Lynchburg for the momentous visit. The Spencers both took to him. He introduced them to other writers and artists, who then invited the Spencers to New York, Washington, and Atlanta, and who would stop at the Spencers' home when their travels brought them to the area.

Few hotels welcomed black travelers in the early 1900s, but even if they had, the Spencers' home was a natural gathering place for many. In addition, Virginia Seminary, lacking suitable facilities, often asked the Spencers to have important visitors as overnight guests.

Among the Spencers' visitors were writers Claude MacKay, W. E. B. DuBois, and Langston Hughes; scientist George Washington Carver, opera singer Paul Robeson, and black leaders Adam Clayton Powell, Thurgood Marshall, Mary McLeod Bethune, and Martin Luther King Jr. Visitors always remarked on Anne's garden and on the hospitality and intellectual stimulation they found at 1313 Pierce Street.

Although H. L. Mencken wrote Anne that her poetry was "ready to print," he and James Weldon Johnson urged her to write prose in addition to poetry. She made an attempt, and even wrote most of a novel, but it was always in poetry that she best expressed herself.

Anne's first published poem was "Before the Feast of Shushan," a dramatic monologue by Persian King Ahasuerus, based on the first book of Esther in the Old Testament. Like most of Anne's poetry, it is universal, for all men and women. In the poem, Vashti is attempting to teach the king that love is important, that women are more than sex objects. The king rejects this new idea, for if he admits that he loves her, then she becomes his equal, which he cannot accept. Johnson sent the poem to Mencken, who wanted her to make changes. She refused, and "Before the Feast of Shushan" was published in 1920 in a magazine called *Crisis*, rather than in a journal edited by Mencken. Even Johnson wanted her to shorten the title, cutting out the first two words, but she stood her ground on that too. The feast mentioned in the title, she stated, never took place. And that was what was significant.

When Anne's first piece of poetry was published, she received a lot of attention locally and nationally, and she was included in the anthology *Negro Poets and Their Poems*, published in 1923 by Robert T. Kerlin. The following year, Louis Untermeyer included Anne's work in *American Poetry Since 1900*. She was published in numerous magazines throughout the 1920s, and Johnson printed five of her poems—including "Before the Feast of Sushan"—in *The Book of American Negro Poetry* in 1922.

In 1925 Alain Locke's *The New Negro* featured Anne's work, and in 1927 ten of her poems were published in Countee Cullen's anthology, *Caroling Dusk*. The *Detroit Free Press*, in reviewing the volume, called Anne a "black Amy Lowell."

Although Anne Spencer wrote more than one hundred poems by her count, only fifty survive, and only thirty were published during her lifetime. She jotted down ideas all day long, on whatever paper was handy—brown grocery bags, the backs of envelopes and letters she'd received, scraps of tablet paper, sometimes even the margins and blank back pages of books she was reading—and put them aside to be worked into poems. She wrote and rewrote, never wanting her work to go out into the world until it was the very best she could make it. Editors became aware of her talent and begged her to submit poems. She usually declined.

Anne sent W. E. B. DuBois some of her poems, which he wanted to enter in a contest, but Anne refused and asked for them back. They were only rough drafts, she said.

Many of the writers of the Harlem Renaissance wrote protest poetry, about "the black experience," because that was mainly what white editors and critics wanted to publish, and black writers had little other opportunity for publication. In addition, publishing was dominated by men, making it doubly hard for a woman to succeed. Anne chose to restrict the number of poems she published rather than compromise her subject matter. She went her own way, writing of gardens, love, death, beauty, and even of such humble subjects as the family laundress and a carnival performer she and Edward witnessed.

Anne considered Central Virginia beautiful in spite of its social problems. One of her poems begins, "Life-long, poor Browning never knew Virginia." Later the poem states, "Heaven's Virginia when the year's at its spring."

Much of Anne's poetry talks of beauty being spoiled by men. Her garden was her sanctuary and solace, a place she and Edward had made beautiful in the midst of a city.

She did write one protest poem, about an Irish man who died after a sixty-four-day hunger strike in a British jail. She submitted it herself to the *Manchester Guardian*. It was rejected, confirming Anne's decision to write her own kind of poetry.

Her mother's second husband had died, so early in the 1920s, she came to live with Anne and her family in Lynchburg, taking over all the cooking duties for the family.

In December 1923 Anne decided she needed a job to supplement Edward's earnings so that their three children—so close in age that they would all be in college at the same time—could be sent north to school. Although she and Edward had met at Virginia Seminary and she felt her life in Lynchburg was good, Anne saw the school's limitations and wanted her children exposed to a wider world than Lynchburg.

For someone who read and wrote poetry, a job in a library would be perfect, she thought. So Anne went to Jones Memorial Library in Lynchburg, carrying along a copy of Johnson's anthology, which included five of her poems. The library was segregated, for whites only, but the administrators hired Anne. She worked a few weeks at the main library until a branch was opened at Dunbar High School. Anne was sent there and worked at Dunbar for the next twenty-two years.

By the early 1940s, Lynchburg officials were pushing Anne to secure credentials as a professional librarian. Standards were being raised in education, and Anne had never taken courses in library science. In fact, she only had a high school education. During the more than two decades she had worked as a librarian at Dunbar, she had never received a raise, earning $75 a month from 1923 until she quit in 1945. On retirement, she received no pension.

Anne produced most of her work during the 1920s, when she was in her forties. The Depression of the 1930s constricted the field of publishing, and Anne's life began to constrict as well. In 1938 James Weldon Johnson, who had been her mentor and friend for two decades, was killed in an automobile accident shortly after leaving the Spencers' home. Anne grieved for him, later writing a poem called "For Jim, Easter Eve," in which she described her garden as a Gethsemane.

A further change came when her mother died in 1947. Her children had grown up, married, and moved away. Old friends had died, and the exciting days of having frequent, stimulating visitors were over. More and more, Anne and Edward spent their time working in their garden and enjoying being alone together.

In the 1950s, schools were integrated across the South. Anne Spencer opposed integration because it so often meant putting a few black students into a white school. The races should live together in harmony in all things, she felt, not merely for a few hours a day in a classroom.

In the 1960s Edward's health began to fail. Several times Anne awoke to find him tucking an imaginary blanket around her. When he died on May 19, 1964, the Lynchburg *News* ran a lengthy editorial praising him as a model citizen.

Losing Edward was devastating to Anne. He had been her husband, lover, friend, and supporter. Shortly after the funeral, Anne went to live with her daughter Bethel, unable to face 1313 Pierce Street without Edward. Within six months she was back in Lynchburg, for Edward's spirit was there, in the house he had built and the garden they had tended together. She seldom left Lynchburg for the remaining decade of her life.

Anne suffered a professional loss when some children broke into Edenkraal, her garden house, and destroyed all her writing stored there.

Anne's children urged her to give up the big house and live with them, or to at least have someone in to take care of her. Bethel even hired a nurse, but Anne fired the woman.

Anne's health deteriorated and her eyesight began to fail. She put aside her other writing and even her notebooks to concentrate on a long poem about John Brown, who was hanged in 1859 for attempting to lead a slave rebellion.

Early in 1974 Anne's work was interrupted by the discovery of a malignancy. She went to New York, where a portion of her tongue was removed and she received chemotherapy. Her speech was slurred thereafter, and she lost weight because it was difficult to eat. In June of that year she wrote a short poem, "1975," convinced that she would die before 1975 ended.

In May 1975, Anne was too ill to attend a ceremony at Virginia University of Lynchburg (the former Virginia Seminary) awarding her an honorary degree. She was the school's oldest living graduate.

Anne Spencer died on July 27, 1975, at age ninety-three. Her home at 1313 Pierce Street is a Virginia Historic Landmark and is listed on the National Register of Historic Places. The house is open by appointment, but the lovely garden is open for enjoyment at all times.

Through the Anne Spencer Foundation, which awards scholarships to promising writers, Anne Spencer is still influencing Lynchburg and the rest of Virginia.

LUCY RANDOLPH MASON

1882–1959

Union Organizer

*L*ucy Mason felt uneasy as she drove into Jackson, Mississippi, in March of 1944. Two representatives of the International Woodworkers of America (an affiliate of the CIO) and the wife of one of the representatives had been arrested and held in jail for thirty-six hours. Their only crime was belonging to a CIO union. Lucy's job was to investigate and, if possible, to make sure no similar arrests were made.

After getting a room at the YWCA, she called on the Bishop of Mississippi. The daughter of a minister, Lucy discovered she had many friends in common with the bishop. As she left to meet the chief of police, the bishop told her she could use his name as a reference.

"I don't think I need a reference, but will you look for me in jail if I disappear?" she later recalled in her autobiography.

"Of course," he promised. "but let's hope it won't come to that."

The chief of police was pleasant, until she told him that she was in Jackson to protect the civil rights of the union members.

He stood and said, "If that's what you want to talk about, you may as well leave."

Lucy Randolph Mason

"I'm sorry, but I can't go until I have your assurance that no more union members will be arrested."

"Why does everybody keep talking to me about civil rights? There's a war on, and I'm just trying to protect our war plants."

Lucy asked what the union members had done to endanger the war plants.

"The CIO people came in like snakes, slipping around at night and hanging around the defense plants. If you go slipping around the plants at night, I'll put you in jail too."

Lucy assured him that she would do no such thing. "I have come here to protect union representatives who are acting under constitutional and legal rights, and in accordance with the National Labor Relations Act. Tell me what these union men must do before they are allowed to talk to the workers." She took out a notebook and pencil to write down what he said.

"You're planning to take down what I say and report to the FBI," he charged. "I won't say anything more until you put away that pencil."

"That's a good idea," Lucy Mason retorted, "but I'll take my charges to the Department of Justice instead, since they ask the FBI to make investigations."

The police chief said that union organizers needed to have an office on the main street so people could see what they were doing, and that they should get a permit from him and permission from the factory manager.

Lucy Mason laughed. Factory managers were unlikely to want unions. She reminded the police chief that he was sworn to uphold the laws and rights of everybody. She left, gave the Justice Department a list of charges, and after a visit from that department, the Jackson police gave the union organizers no more trouble.

Jackson, Mississippi, represented one of Lucy's successes, deflecting violence away from organizers seeking better working conditions for poor Southerners. As she said, "Not many people will shoot or beat a little white-haired woman." There were failures too, workplaces that remained sweatshops, but it was not for her lack of trying.

Lucy Randolph Mason was born on July 26, 1882, in a house called Clarens, on the grounds of the Episcopal Seminary in Alexandria, Virginia. Her father, Reverend Landon Randolph Mason, was an Episcopal priest in Shepherdstown, West Virginia. Her mother, Lucy Ambler Mason, had gone to stay with her sisters in Alexandria for the birth of the baby.

Lucy was descended from some of Virginia's most eminent citizens. Her great-great-great-grandfather was George Mason, author of Virginia's Declaration of Rights, a forerunner of the U.S. Bill of Rights. Three of her ancestors had signed the Declaration of Independence, and her mother's great-great-uncle was Supreme Court Justice John Marshall. Her great-grandfather had been Confederate envoy to Great Britain. Relatives included Robert E. Lee and numerous Randolphs, Carters, Bollings, and Amblers—prominent names in Virginia history.

But distinguished lineage and a tradition of seeking rights didn't pay the bills. The Masons were poor. Her father's first parish church was in Drake's Branch, a village in southern Virginia, where he was paid $500 a year. Much of it, her mother said, was paid in bacon and black-eyed peas.

The family moved first to Shepherdstown, then to Georgia, and then to Richmond, Virginia, where the Reverend Mason was paid $2,400 a year and was furnished with a house. Mrs. Mason taught a Bible class at the nearby state penitentiary, and the family often took in as guests newly released prisoners who were looking for work and trying to make a fresh start. Getting work that paid enough to support a family was difficult then for prisoners and other workers. Virginia, like the rest of the defeated South, was desperately poor.

The family managed to send Lucy's brothers to the University of Virginia, but because girls were seldom educated beyond secondary school, Lucy did not attend college. Her sister married a banker and moved from Richmond to Alexandria, but Lucy never wed. Although as a teenager she planned to be a missionary, she soon decided to stay in Virginia, get a job to help with family finances, and do good work right in her own area.

When Lucy was twenty-two she rented a typewriter, taught herself to type and write shorthand, and got a job paying five dollars a week. Within two years she was earning $75 a month as a stenographer for corporation lawyer Allen Braxton. When Braxton died in 1914, the law firm was dissolved, and Lucy accepted a job as industrial secretary at the Young Women's Christian Association. She loved working for the YWCA and held the job for four years, until several family tragedies changed the course of her life.

Her mother died suddenly in January 1918 of a heart attack, and her brother was killed in the war in France later that year. Her father, age seventy-six, recently retired, and hard of hearing, was almost blind from cataracts. Clearly, someone had to take care of him. Lucy's sister had family responsibilities, as did her brother John, an engineer who lived with his family in Baltimore. Her younger brother was away fighting in the British army. Lucy would be the caregiver, with financial support from her brother John.

Lucy gave up her job at the YWCA and cared for her father for five and a half years until his death. Two of her friends who lived in the Mason house stayed with the Reverend Mason occasionally so Lucy could do volunteer work.

All around her in Richmond she saw how poorly most workers were treated, and how much better off union workers were. The latter had eight-hour days and half of Saturday off, while nonunion workers put in ten- and eleven-hour days six days a week. Lucy became president of the League of Women Voters, joined the

Union Label League, whose purpose was to promote the purchase of clothing made by union members, and walked in the snow to support striking streetcar workers.

After her father's death in 1923, Lucy again worked for the YWCA, this time as general secretary. She was offered a job as southern secretary of the National Consumers League, a position she found very appealing, as she would be promoting social and labor legislation. But she had given her word to the YWCA that she would be its secretary for a year. And there was much work to be done in Richmond.

Florence Kelley, general secretary of the Consumers League, wrote that Lucy was wasting her time and energy on less important matters. Working for the Consumers League, she wrote, Lucy could help modernize the Supreme Court and the U.S. Constitution. But Kelley recognized Lucy's integrity in continuing with the job she had accepted and said the League would wait a year for her. But nine years passed before Lucy accepted a position with the Consumers League, and then it was as Kelley's successor.

In 1931 Lucy was part of a delegation that traveled about the South trying to build support for improved hours and working conditions for women and children. During the depths of the Depression, with millions unemployed, mill owners could pick and choose among workers and set their own pay scales. This was especially true in textile manufacturing. In the late 1920s, factories had overproduced, warehouses were full, and prices dropped disastrously. Mill owners were in danger of going bankrupt. In 1928 they formed the Cotton Textile Institute, which aimed for a voluntary reduction of workers' hours with no cut in pay. This worked for a while, but then some mills began to increase workers' hours to produce more cloth, which defeated the purpose.

A few factory owners supported national labor laws. This would mean that all mills would treat their workers the same, so the competition would be fair. A bill was introduced in Congress for a universal eight-hour day, with no night work for women or workers under eighteen. It failed to pass, but it formed the basis of later labor laws.

After two months of traveling about the South, Lucy returned to Richmond and wrote a pamphlet, *Standards for Workers in Southern Industry*. Printed by the Consumers League, it was to have far-reaching effects. The Cotton Textile Institute distributed 500 copies among manufacturers, using it as a threat: If the voluntary agreement to improve hours and conditions was not complied with, the government would pass compulsory laws. Two years later, Secretary of Labor Frances Perkins distributed the pamphlet at the National Labor Legislation Conference.

The Consumers League had been founded to investigate the conditions under which consumer goods were produced and to educate buyers about those often inhumane conditions. Consumers could then boycott offending manufacturers, or work for laws to change the conditions. After Florence Kelley's death, Lucy Mason was chosen to head up the organization because she could be effective in the South, where conditions were especially bad. Ironically, Lucy had to move to New York to take the position.

By 1932 wages had plummeted in New York as well as in the impoverished South. When a garment manufacturer advertised for skilled workers at $10 a week, police had to break up the ensuing riot as women fought for the jobs.

In Washington, President Franklin Roosevelt had called a group of commissioners to set National Recovery Administration Codes, regulations to stimulate the economy. Lucy Mason testified before the commissioners in the summer of 1933 for the unorganized industries. When she was asked what textile workers would do with more money if their wages were raised, she answered, "They would spend it on more and better food, on shoes so their children can attend school in winter, on better clothes. They might even go to a movie once in a while, or buy an old car and some gasoline and visit their people. In short, they would do with their higher pay exactly what President Roosevelt hopes they will do— spend it and create more business for everyone."

She was greeted with laughter and applause.

When Lucy testified about wages in the stone and gravel industry, she was told that if blacks, who made up most of the workers in that industry, were paid twenty-five cents per hour, they would work only a few days each week and laze the rest of the time. Nonsense, she answered. Black workers had the same need to support their families that whites did.

Her testimony and reports were important in passage of the Fair Labor Standards Act, which finally became law in 1938, setting an eight-hour day, a forty-hour week, and a minimum wage that could be adjusted upward with an improving economy.

Despite her successes in the North, Lucy wanted to return to the South, to ensure that the new laws were carried out for the benefit of the workers. Her sister suggested she ask John L. Lewis, president of the American Federation of Labor, for a job. Lewis was impressed that she wanted to work in the South, where much organizing was needed, and suggested that she work as a publicist and public relations representative for the CIO, especially the Textile Workers Organizing Committee. Lucy said she'd been making $5,000 a year working for the Consumers League, but would accept the $3,600 salary she'd earned as general secretary for the YWCA. Lewis offered the $5,000, but she said she didn't want to make so much more than the workers. She was paid $3,600, which was raised to $4,000 in 1945, still a handsome sum for that period.

Some accused Lucy of being a "traitor to her class," but she saw it as her duty to improve conditions for all Southerners. She used her status, knowing that men of all categories would hesitate to attack a genteel Southern woman. A man might have been beaten in the night, but not a woman, and especially not a minister's daughter. Too, she knew many influential people all over the South, and was kin to many of them. She used connections, friends they had in common, and that old standby, Southern charm.

In one Virginia textile town, the union had been voted down twice. Before the third election, "Miss Lucy" was sent in to find out who had power, and to butter him up. She talked to first one and then another of the town's influential men. Finally one asked, "Who sent you? And who are you anyway?" She regaled him with a long list of her ancestors and all they'd done to secure rights for Americans. When she finished, he said, "Lady, I don't know what they're paying you, but whatever it is, you're worth it."

Not all her encounters were as peaceful. In Huntsville, Alabama, Merrimack Mills laid off many workers in the autumn of 1937, which increased the workload on the others. The mill then closed in November, and when it reopened in April 1938, new workers were hired. Huntsville was a company town, with workers living in company housing, banking at the company bank, and shopping at company-owned stores. If the union members were not rehired, they would be destitute, for the company structure left little of their wages to be saved. Unemployed workers were evicted from company-owned houses, and when the unions picketed the factory, the town newspaper warned that they would be blacklisted so no factory in America would hire them.

Lucy approached Birmingham newspapers and was able to get editorials printed that were favorable to unions. Then she attended a conference at which Eleanor Roosevelt was the speaker. Lucy sent a note asking to speak with Mrs. Roosevelt; after her speech, the president's wife heard of the plight of the Huntsville workers. She promised to speak to the president, who sent in representatives of the National Labor Relations Board to remedy the situation. The evictions were stopped, and the union secured a contract with the mill.

Miss Lucy didn't always succeed. Union organizers had been driven out of a certain town three times. Even another union woman had failed to bring labor peace, and had had to pack and leave town hurriedly. The southern director of the Amalgamated Clothing Workers of America wrote Lucy asking her to go have a try. She drove into town in her trusty Plymouth and parked in front of the bank.

Probably thinking the pleasant Virginia woman had come to open an account, the banker received her graciously. They chatted amiably after she told him her brother-in-law was a banker. When he discovered Lucy was in town on union business, he furiously told her what he thought of unions and the government: "If the government in Washington under this crazy New Deal passes laws that this town disapproves, the thing for us and other towns to do is to ignore them. We are law-abiding people. We sleep with our doors unlocked, but we keep a pistol on the table beside our bed. The Labor Board is unfair and should be disregarded until Congress wipes it out."

Her next visit was to the local judge, who was also on the antiunion committee. Having been alerted by the banker, he walked away from her after declaring, "I'm not going to talk about the damned CIO. I am against it and am going to do all I can to get it out of here."

Lucy then went to the mayor's office, but the mayor was out of town. She talked instead to his brother, a young lawyer who was sympathetic to the union cause. He told her, however, that the town had given a subsidy to the garment-makers to build a factory there and had promised them "no union trouble."

"I advise you to leave town before nightfall. I don't think the antiunion committee will harm you, but tensions are high, and anything can happen," he said. Lucy left, conceding defeat there.

Memphis had both large and small plants, and the boss of the whole area, a Democratic National Committeeman, had made an agreement with the American Federation of Labor (AFL) that if they would cease organizing large plants, he would protect their organization of craft unions. Memphis wanted to attract large industries by promising nonunion labor. The CIO was not part of the agreement, however, and went about organizing workers in the large plants. The CIO was especially effective because it accepted black as well as white workers.

By 1940 there was constant conflict between the city and the AFL on one side and the CIO on the other. Workers were threatened, cars were overturned and burned, newspaper editors took sides, and organizers were refused hotel rooms and apartments. Lucy attempted to talk to the city boss, but he evaded her. She realized she could use his political position against him. Leaving Memphis, she wrote Eleanor Roosevelt for help. Mrs. Roosevelt suggested a lunch meeting in New York, where Lucy told her all that was going on in Memphis, emphasizing that the boss was turning workers against the Democratic Party by his actions against the unions. Mrs. Roosevelt asked Lucy to write a report for the president and promised to see that it was put on his bedside table.

Within a few weeks, a special representative of the U.S. Attorney General appeared in Memphis and talked with various city officials. They denied that they had interfered with workers' civil rights and vowed that there would be no such violations in the future. There weren't, and union membership grew rapidly in Memphis.

In Tifton, Georgia, in 1948, Lucy was able to avert violence during a strike of meat packers. She arrived by train on a Sunday evening, talked to the local union organizers, and went to her hotel for the night. The next morning she was called to witness a black striker who had been beaten in the night by the sheriff and a plant guard. After getting the man's statement and writing a report for the Civil Rights Section of the Justice Department, Lucy went to the judge's office and told him the story. He said he'd have the sheriff report to his office that afternoon at four.

Lucy arrived at four too. The sheriff's office was across the hall from the judge's, and in the hall the sheriff and three deputies, all armed, faced off against three unarmed union organizers. The sheriff cursed the union organizers, calling them white trash. One organizer charged the sheriff, but Lucy stepped between them and laughed, turning the matter into a joke. Placing her hands on the organizers' shoulders, with her back to the sheriff, she kept smiling and pushing the men out to the street. The sheriff followed, reluctant to pull Lucy aside. She persuaded the organizers to get in their car and leave, and she stayed with the four law officers, who sheepishly put away their guns, unwilling to be seen attacking or arresting a much-outnumbered little white-haired woman.

By the time Lucy Randolph Mason retired from the CIO in 1952, she had seen solid gains socially, financially, and psychologically for both blacks and whites in the South. The races were getting accustomed to working together, accepting each other, and voting for each other, for the good of all.

Lucy Randolph Mason wrote her autobiography, *To Win These Rights*, later that year. Six years later, in 1959, she died in Atlanta, Georgia.

BIBLIOGRAPHY

GENERAL

Dabney, Virginius. *Virginia, The New Dominion.* New York: Doubleday & Company, 1971.

Frank, Sid. *The Presidents: Tidbits and Trivia.* Maplewood, N.J.: Hammond, Inc., 1975.

Garraty, John A. *The American Nation.* New York: Harper & Row, 1966.

Klapthor, Margaret Brown. *First Ladies Cookbook.* New York: Parents Magazine Press, 1965.

McConnell, Jane, and Burt McConnell. *Our First Ladies.* New York: Thomas Crowell, 1964.

Truman, Margaret. *First Ladies.* New York: Random House, 1995.

POCAHONTAS

Adams, Patricia. *The Story of Pocahontas, Indian Princess.* Milwaukee, Wisc.: Gareth Stevens Publishing Company, 1987.

Barker-Benfield, G. J., and Catherine Clinton. *Portraits of American Women from Settlement to the Present.* New York: St. Martin's Press, 1991.

Fishwick, Marshall. "Was John Smith a Liar?" *American Heritage* IX, no. 6 (October 1958): 28–33, 110–111.

Fritz, Jean. *The Double Life of Pocahontas.* Lakeville, Conn.: Grey Castle Press, 1983.

Rountree, Helen C. *Pocahontas's People.* Norman, Okla.: University of Oklahoma Press, 1990.

Watson, Virginia. *The Legend of Pocahontas.* New York: Avenel Publishing Company, 1995.

Woodward, Grace Steele. *Pocahontas.* Norman, Okla.: University of Oklahoma Press, 1963.

MARTHA WASHINGTON

Bourne, Miriam Anne. *First Family: George Washington and His Intimate Relations.* New York: W. W. Norton & Company, 1982.

Boyd, Thomas M. "Death of a Hero, Death of a Friend—George Washington's Last Hours." *Virginia Cavalcade* XXXIII, no. 3 (Winter 1984): 136–138.

Brooks, Geraldine. *Dames & Daughters of Colonial Days.* New York: Arno Press, 1974.

Moore, Charles. *The Family Life of George Washington.* Boston: Houghton Mifflin, 1926.

Logan, Mrs. John. *The Part Taken by Women in American History.* Wilmington, Del.: Perry-Nolle Publishing Company, 1912.

Rinaldi, Nicholas. "George Washington at Home in Virginia." *Early American Life* VIII, no. I, (February 1977): 11–17.

Thane, Elswyth. *Washington's Lady.* New York: Curtis Publishing Company, 1954.

Vance, Marguerite. *Martha, Daughter of Virginia.* New York: E. P. Dutton & Company, 1947.

ELIZABETH HENRY RUSSELL

Armistead, Mary B. "Pioneer, Colonial Women Make Big Contrast," *Roanoke Times,* 4 July 1976, 22.

Asbury, Francis. *Journal of Rev. Francis Asbury.* New York: Lane & Scott Publishing Company, 1852.

Blackwell, Mack J. Jr. *The Preston Salt Works: A Vital Link to Southwest Virginia's Industrial Beginning.* Privately published by the author at Abingdon, VA, 1992.

Catron, Jerry. Interview by author. Madame Russell House, Saltville, Va. 6 June 2001.

Preston, Nelly C. *Paths of Glory.* Richmond, Va.: Whittet & Shepperson, 1961.

Preston, Thomas L. *A Sketch of Mrs. Elizabeth Russell, Wife of General William Campbell, Sister of Patrick Henry.* Nashville, Tenn.: Publishing House of the Methodist Episcopal Church, 1888.

Runyan, Elva. "Patrick Henry's Sister, 'the Veriest Sinner Upon the Earth' and Madame Russell, Methodist Saint." Master's thesis, University of Virginia, 1941.

Summers, Lewis Preston. *History of Southwest Virginia and Washington County.* Baltimore, Md.: Regional Publishing Company, 1979.

DOLLEY MADISON

Britton, Rick. "Dolley Madison at Montpelier," *Albemarle* no. 80 (February-March 2001): 51–54.

Gerson, Noel B. *The Velvet Glove, A Life of Dolly Madison.* Nashville, Tenn.: Thomas Nelson, 1975.

Logan, Mrs. John. *The Part Taken by Women in American History.* Wilmington, Del.: Perry-Nolle Publishing Company, 1912.

Lord, Walter. *The Dawn's Early Light.* New York: Dell, 1972.

Montpelier Foundation. *"James Madison's Montpelier."* Montpelier Station, Va.: Montpelier Foundation, 2002.

Nolan, Jeannette Covert. *Dolley Madison.* New York: Julian Messner, 1958.

Truman, Margaret. *Women of Courage.* New York: William Morrow, 1976.

Wilson, Dorothy Clarke. *Queen Dolley: The Life and Times of Dolley Madison.* Garden City, N.Y.: Doubleday, 1987.

ANNE NEWPORT ROYALL

Dexter, Elizabeth Anthony. *Career Women of America 1776–1840.* Boston: Houghton Mifflin, 1950.

Douglas, Emily Taft. "Printer's Ink & Greasepaint," in *Remember the Ladies.* New York: G. P. Putnam's Sons, 1966.

Forbes, Malcolm. "Anne Newport Royall: the First Female American Journalist," in *Women Who Made a Difference.* New York: Simon & Schuster, 1990.

James, Bessie Rowland. *Anne Royall's USA*. New Brunswick, N.J.: Rutgers University Press, 1972.

Sawyers, Susan. "Visiting Writer Liked What She Saw in Lynchburg," in *Tales of the Hill City*. Lynchburg, Va.: Carter Glass Newspapers, 1985.

Watson, Lucille McWane. "Lynchburg's First Historical: Anne Royall, Pioneer Journalist." *The Iron Worker* 20 (Winter 1955–56): 6–13.

PRISCILLA COOPER TYLER

Coleman, Elizabeth Tyler. *Priscilla Cooper Tyler*. University, Ala.: University of Alabama Press, 1955.

Cunningham, Homer F. "John Tyler," in *The Presidents' Last Years*. Jefferson, N.C.: McFarland and Company, 1989.

Mann, Nancy Wilson. *Tylers and Gardiners on the Village Green*. New York: Vantage Press, 1983.

Peterson, Helen Stone. "First Lady at 22," *Virginia Cavalcade* XI., no. 3 (Winter 1961–62): 14–21.

Peterson, Norma Lewis. *The Presidencies of William Henry Harrison and John Tyler*. Laurence: University Press of Kansas, 1989.

Shockley, Martin Staples. "Priscilla Cooper in the Richmond Theater." *Virginia Magazine of History and Biography* 67 (1959): 180–185.

Speidell, Phyllis. "Sherwood Forest." *Virginian Pilot*, 2 September 2001, sec. E, p. 1.

BELLE BOYD AND ELIZABETH VAN LEW

Garrison, Webb. *A Treasury of Virginia Tales*. Nashville, Tenn.: Rutledge Hill Press, 1991.

Hoehling, A. A., and Mary Hoehling. *The Day Richmond Died*. New York: A. S. Barnes and Company, 1981.

————. *Women Who Spied*. New York: Dodd, Mead, 1967.

Massey, Mary Elizabeth. *Bonnet Brigades—American Women and the Civil War*. New York: Alfred A. Knopf, 1966.

Sigaud, Louis A. *Belle Boyd, Confederate Spy*. Richmond, Va.: Dietz Press, 1944.

Tucker, George. "Belle a Woman of Intrigue and Also Three Husbands," *Virginian Pilot*, 6 May 2001, sec. B, p. 3.

Turney, Catherine. "Crazy Betty," *Mankind* III, no. 3, (October 1971): 58–64.

Van Lew, Elizabeth. *A Yankee Spy in Richmond: The Civil War Diary of "Crazy Bet" Van Lew*. Edited by David D. Ryan. Mechanicsburg, Pa.: Stackpole Books, 1996.

MAGGIE LENA WALKER

African American Reference Library. "Maggie L. Walker," in *African American Biography*. Detroit: U.X.L, 1994.

Branch, Muriel Miller, and Dorothy Marie Rice. *Pennies to Dollars*. Richmond, Va.: Marlborough House, 1984.

Hine, Darlene Clark, ed. *Black Women in America, the Early Years 1619–1899*. New York: Facts on File, 1997.

Koslow, Philip. "Maggie Walker," in *African American Reference*. New York: New York Public Library, Schomburg Center for Research in Black Culture, 1999.

Longwell, Marjorie. "Maggie Lena Walker," In *America and Women*. Philadelphia: Dorrance and Company, 1962.

"Negro Leader's Rites Arranged," *Richmond News Leader*, 17 December 1934.

Pettiger, Betty. "Maggie Walker House: Park Service to the Rescue," *Richmond Times Dispatch*, 28 July 1981.

Smith, Jessie Carney, ed. "Maggie L. Walker," in *Notable Black American Women*. Detroit: Gale Research, 1991.

White, Pam. "Famous Grandma Walker was 'Full of Fun,'" *Richmond News Leader*, 16 July 1979.

EDITH BOLLING WILSON

Archer, Jules. *World Citizen, Woodrow Wilson*. New York: Julian Messner, 1967.

Cunningham, Homer F. "The 28th, Woodrow Wilson," in *The Presidents' Last Years*. Jefferson, N.C.: McFarland and Company, 1989.

Forbes, Malcolm. "Edith Bolling Wilson," in *Women Who Made a Difference*. New York: Simon and Schuster, 1990.

Hatch, Alden. *Edith Bolling Wilson, First Lady Extraordinary*. New York: Dodd, Mead, 1961.

Link, Arthur S. *Woodrow Wilson, A Brief Biography*. Chicago: Quadrangle Books, 1963.

Smith, Gene. *When the Cheering Stopped*. New York: William Morrow, 1964.

Wilson, Edith Bolling. *My Memoir*. New York: Bobbs-Merrill, 1938.

"Woodrow Wilson," *The American Experience*. PBS Television, 13 January 2002.

ELLEN GLASGOW

Dabney, Virginius. *Richmond, The Story of a City*. Charlottesville, Va.: University Press of Virginia, 1990.

Glasgow, Ellen. *Barren Ground*. New York: Harcourt, Brace, 1925.

————. *Letters of Ellen Glasgow*. Edited by Blair Rouse. New York: Harcourt, Brace, 1958.

————. *The Sheltered Life*. New York: Harcourt, Brace, 1938.

————. *The Woman Within*. New York: Harcourt, Brace, 1954.

Holman, C. Hugh. *Three Modes of Modern Southern Fiction*. Athens, Ga.: University of Georgia Press, 1966.

McDowell, Frederick P. W. *Ellen Glasgow and the Ironic Art of Fiction*. Madison, Wisc.: University of Wisconsin Press, 1963.

Simonini, R. C. Jr. *Southern Writers—Appraisals in Our Time*. Charlottesville, Va.: University Press of Virginia, 1958.

NANCY LANGHORNE ASTOR

Balsan, Consuelo Vanderbilt. *The Glitter and the Gold*. Maidstone, England: George Mann Publishing, 1973.

Fox, James. *Five Sisters—The Langhornes of Virginia*. New York: Simon and Schuster, 2000.

Grigg, John. *Nancy Astor, A Lady Unashamed.* Boston: Little, Brown and Co., 1980.

Langhorne, Elizabeth. *Nancy Astor and Her Friends.* New York: Praeger Publishers, 1974.

Sinclair, David. *Dynasty: The Astors and Their Times.* London: J. M. Dent and Sons, 1983.

Sykes, Christopher. *Nancy—The Life of Lady Astor.* New York: Harper and Row, 1972.

ANNE SPENCER

Barksdale, Richard, and Kenneth Kinnamon. *Black Writers of America.* New York: Macmillan, 1972.

Greene, J. Lee. "Anne Spencer of Lynchburg," *Virginia Cavalcade* XXVII, no. 4, (Spring 1978): 178–183.

———. *Time's Unfolding Garden: Anne Spencer's Life and Poetry.* Baton Rouge: Louisiana State University Press, 1977.

Hine, Darlene Clark, ed. "Anne Spencer," in *Black Women in America.* New York: Facts on File, 1997.

Honey, Maureen, ed. *Shadowed Dreams: Women's Poetry of the Harlem Renaissance.* New Brunswick, N.J.: Rutgers University Press, 1989.

Laurant, Darrell. "Feisty Anne Spencer Produced Fine Poetry," in *Tales of the Hill City.* Lynchburg, Va.: Carter Glass Newspapers, 1985.

Lynchburg Regional Convention and Visitors Bureau. *Explore Our Legacy—A Guide to African American Heritage.* Lynchburg, Va.: Lynchburg Regional Convention and Visitors Bureau, 2001.

Salem, Dorothy, ed. "Anne Spencer," in *African American Women.* New York: Garland Publishing, 1993.

Smith, Jessie Carney, ed. "Anne Spencer," in *Notable Black American Women.* Detroit: Gale Research, 1991.

LUCY RANDOLPH MASON

Atlanta Constitution, 7 May 1959. Obituary.

Brooks, Thomas. *Toil and Trouble, A History of American Labor.* New York: Delacorte, 1964.

Fink, Gary M. *Biographical Dictionary of American Labor.* Westport, Conn.: Greenwood Press, 1990.

Lader, Lawrence. "The Lady and the Sheriff," *The New Republic,* 5 January 1948: 17–19.

Mason, Lucy Randolph. *To Win These Rights.* New York: Harper and Brothers, 1952.

New York Times, 8 May 1959. Obituary.

O'Farrell, Brigid, and Joyce L. Kornbluh, eds. *Rocking the Boat: Union Women's Voices, 1915–1975.* New Brunswick, N.J.: Rutgers University Press, 1996.

"Lucy Randolph Mason papers" in *Operation Dixie: The CIO Organizing Committee Papers, 1946–1953.* Sanford, N.C.: Microfilming Corporation of America, 1980.

Salmond, John A. *Miss Lucy of the CIO—The Life and Times of Lucy Randolph Mason 1882—1959.* Athens, Ga.: University of Georgia Press, 1988.

Sicherman, Barbara, and Carol Hurd Green, eds. *Notable American Women of the Modern Period.* Cambridge, Mass.: Belknap Press of Harvard University, 1980.

Virginia Biographical Dictionary. New York: Somerset Publishing, 1993.

$\mathcal{J}$NDEX

Index

About the Author

Emilee Hines is a native Virginian with a deep interest in the history of her state and its people. She is a graduate of Lynchburg College and has a master's degree in history from the University of North Carolina in Chapel Hill. She has taught in Virginia and in Kenya. Her published writing includes *It Happened in Virginia*, seven volumes of *Old Virginia Houses*, and more than 250 articles and short stories.

Emilee is married to Thomas B. Cantieri, and they live in Portsmouth, Virginia. They have a daughter, Catherine.